Avigail Schimmel

CHARLES WRIGHT

NEGATIVE BLUE

CHARLES WRIGHT was born in Pickwick Dam, Tennessee, in
1935. His work has most recently been collected in *The World
of the Ten Thousand Things: Poems 1980–1990* (FSG, 1990). He
received the Academy of American Poets' Lenore Marshall
Poetry Prize for *Chickamauga* in 1996; in 1998 he received the
Pulitzer Prize for Poetry and the National Book Critics Circle
Award for *Black Zodiac*. Wright's many other awards include the
Ruth Lilly Poetry Prize in 1993, the Award of Merit Medal from
the American Academy of Arts and Letters in 1992, and the 1979
PEN Translation Prize for his version of Eugenio Montale's *The
Storm and Other Things*. He teaches at the University of Virginia
in Charlottesville.

NEGATIVE BLUE

NEGATIVE BLUE

Selected Later Poems

CHARLES WRIGHT

FARRAR, STRAUS AND GIROUX

NEW YORK

FARRAR, STRAUS AND GIROUX

Printed in the United States of America
Published in 2000 by Farrar, Straus & Giroux
First paperback edition, 2001

Grateful acknowledgment is made to the following publications, in whose pages these poems first appeared: *The American Poetry Review, The Amicus Journal, Antaeus, The Atlanta Review, The Bellingham Review, The Bitter Oleander, The Bread Loaf Anthology, The Carolina Quarterly, The Colorado Review, Columbia, DoubleTake, Excerpt, Field, Five Points, The Gettysburg Review, Grand Street, Green Mountain Review, The Iron Mountain Review, The Iowa Review, The Kenyon Review, Meridan, The Michigan Quarterly Review, The Nation, The New England Review, The New Yorker, The New Republic, The Ohio Review, Orion, The Oxford American, The Paris Review, The Partisan Review, Ploughshares, Poetry, The Recorder, River City, Shenandoah, Slate, The Southern Review, The Southwest Review, Sycamore, Thornwillow, The Threepenny Review, Virginia Quarterly Review, The Wallace Stevens Journal, Western Humanities Review,* and *The Yale Review.* "Still Life with Stick and Word" appeared in a book published by The Windhover Press for the University of Iowa Museum, "Summer Storm" appeared in *Transforming Vision,* published by The Art Institute of Chicago and Bullfinch Press, and "North American Bear" was published in a small press edition titled *North American Bear* by Sutton Hoo Press in 1999.

Library of Congress Cataloging-in-Publication Data
Wright, Charles, 1935–
   Negative blue : selected later poems / Charles Wright.
   p.   cm.
   ISBN 0-374-52773-3 (pbk.)
   I. Title.
PS3573.R52N44   2000
811′.54—dc21   99-36987

Designed by Gretchen Achilles

CONTENTS

CHICKAMAUGA

SITTING OUTSIDE AT THE END OF AUTUMN

Three years ago, in the afternoons,
                    I used to sit back here and try
To answer the simple arithmetic of my life,
But never could figure it—
This object and that object
Never contained the landscape
                              nor all of its implications,
This tree and that shrub
Never completely satisfied the sum or quotient
I took from or carried to,
                    nor do they do so now,
Though I'm back here again, looking to calculate,
Looking to see what adds up.

Everything comes from something,
                    only something comes from nothing,
Lao Tzu says, more or less.
Eminently sensible, I say,
Rubbing this tiny snail shell between my thumb and two fingers.
Delicate as an earring,
                    it carries its emptiness like a child
It would be rid of.
I rub it clockwise and counterclockwise, hoping for anything
Resplendent in its vocabulary or disguise—
But one and one make nothing, he adds,
                              endless and everywhere,
The shadow that everything casts.

READING LAO TZU AGAIN IN THE NEW YEAR

Snub end of a dismal year,
                              deep in the dwarf orchard,
The sky with its undercoat of blackwash and point stars,
I stand in the dark and answer to
My life, this shirt I want to take off,
                              which is on fire . . .

Old year, new year, old song, new song,
                              nothing will change hands
Each time we change heart, each time
Like a hard cloud that has drifted all day through the sky
Toward the night's shrugged shoulder
                              with its epaulet of stars.

———————

Prosodies rise and fall.
                    Structures rise in the mind and fall.
Failure reseeds the old ground.
Does the grass, with its inches in two worlds, love the dirt?
Does the snowflake the raindrop?

I've heard that those who know will never tell us,
                              and heard
That those who tell us will never know.
Words are wrong.
Structures are wrong.
                    Even the questions are compromise.

4

Desire discriminates and language discriminates:
They form no part of the essence of all things:

                                  each word
Is a failure, each object
We name and place
                leads us another step away from the light.

Loss is its own gain.
                Its secret is emptiness.
Our images lie in the flat pools of their dark selves
Like bodies of water the tide moves.
They move as the tide moves.
                      Its secret is emptiness.

————

Four days into January,
                  the grass grows tiny, tiny
Under the peach trees.
Wind from the Blue Ridge tumbles the hat
Of daylight farther and farther
                    into the eastern counties.

Sunlight spray on the ash limbs.
                  Two birds
Whistle at something unseen, one black note and one interval.
We're placed between now and not-now,
                      held by affection,
Large rock balanced upon a small rock.

UNDER THE NINE TREES IN JANUARY

Last night's stars and last night's wind
Are west of the mountains now, and east of the river.
Here, under the branches of the nine trees,
                how small the world seems.

Should we lament, in winter, our shadow's solitude,
Our names spelled out like snowflakes?
Where is it written, *the season's decrease diminishes me?*

Should we long for stillness,
                a hush for the trivial body
Washed in the colors of paradise,
Dirt-colored water-colored match-flame-and-wind-colored?

As one who has never understood the void,
                should I
Give counsel to the darkness, honor the condor's wing?
Should we keep on bowing to
                an inch of this and an inch of that?

The world is a handkerchief.
Today I spread it across my knees.
Tomorrow they'll fold it into my breast pocket,
                white on my dark suit.

AFTER READING WANG WEI,
I GO OUTSIDE TO THE FULL MOON

Back here, old snow like lace cakes,
Candescent and brittle now and then through the tall grass.
Remorse, remorse, the dark drones.

The body's the affliction,
No resting place in the black pews of the winter trees,
No resting place in the clouds.

Mercy upon us, old man,
You in the China dust, I this side of my past life,
Salt in the light of heaven.

Isolate landscape. World's grip.
The absolute, as small as a poker chip, moves off,
Bright moon shining between pines.

EASTER 1989

March is the month of slow fire,
                              new grasses stung with rain,
Cold-shouldered, white-lipped.
Druidic crocus circles appear
Overnight, morose in their purple habits,
                              wet cowls
Glistening in the cut sun.

Instinct will end us.
The force that measles the peach tree
                              will divest and undo us.
The power that kicks on
                    the cells in the lilac bush
Will tumble us down and down.
Under the quince tree, purple cross points, and that's all right

For the time being,
                    the willow across the back fence
Menacing in its green caul.
When the full moon comes
                              gunning under the cloud's cassock
Later tonight, the stations
Will start to break forth like stars, their numbers flashing and then some.

Belief is a paltry thing
                    and will betray us, soul's load scotched
Against the invisible.
We are what we've always thought we were—

Peeling the membrane back,

                        amazed, like the jonquil's yellow head

Butting the nothingness—

                   in the wrong place, in the wrong body.

The definer of all things

                cannot be spoken of.

It is not knowledge or truth.

We get no closer than next-to-it.

Beyond wisdom, beyond denial,

                    it asks us for nothing,

According to Pseudo-Dionysus, which sounds good to me.

———————

Nubbly with enzymes,

The hardwoods gurgle and boil in their leathery sheaths.

Flame flicks the peony's fuse.

Out of the caves of their locked beings,

                    fluorescent shapes

Roll the darkness aside as they rise to enter the real world.

READING RORTY AND PAUL CELAN
ONE MORNING IN EARLY JUNE

In the skylight it's Sunday,
A little aura between the slats of the Venetian blinds.
Outside the front window,
                        a mockingbird balances
Gingerly on a spruce branch.
At the Munch house across the street,
Rebecca reads through the paper, then stares at her knees
On the front porch.
                        Church bell. Weed-eater's cough and spin.

From here, the color of mountains both is and is not,
Beginning of June,
Haze like a nesting bird in the trees,
The Blue Ridge partial,
                        then not partial,
Between the staff lines of the telephone wires and pine tips
That sizzle like E.T.'s finger.
Mid-nineties, and summer officially still three weeks away.

                    ————————

If truth is made and not found,
                        what an amazing world
We live in, more secret than ever
And beautiful of access.
Goodbye, old exits, goodbye, old entrances, the way
Out is the way in at last,
Two-hearted sorrow of middle age,
                                substanceless blue,
Benevolent anarchy to tan and grow old with.

If sentences constitute
                    everything we believe,
Vocabularies retool
Our inability to measure and get it right,
And languages don't exist.
That's one theory. Here's another:
Something weighs on our shoulders
And settles itself like black light
                    invisibly in our hair . . .

———————

Pool table. Zebra rug.
                    Three chairs in a half circle.
Buck horns and Ca' Paruta.
Gouache of the Clinchfield station in Kingsport, Tennessee.
High tide on the Grand Canal,
                    San Zeno in late spring
Taken by "Ponti" back in the nineteenth century.
I see the unknown photographer
                    under his dark cloth. Magnesium flash.
Silence. I hear what he has to say.

June 3rd, heat like Scotch tape on the skin,
Mountains the color of nothing again,
                    then something through mist.
In Tuscany, on the Sette Ponti, Gròpina dead-ends
Above the plain and the Arno's marauding cities,
Columns eaten by darkness,
Cathedral unsentenced and plugged in
To what's-not-there,
                    windows of alabaster, windows of flame.

AFTER READING TU FU, I GO OUTSIDE TO THE DWARF ORCHARD

East of me, west of me, full summer.
How deeper than elsewhere the dusk is in your own yard.
Birds fly back and forth across the lawn
                                    looking for home
As night drifts up like a little boat.

Day after day, I become of less use to myself.
Like this mockingbird,
                    I flit from one thing to the next.
What do I have to look forward to at fifty-four?
Tomorrow is dark.
                Day-after-tomorrow is darker still.

The sky dogs are whimpering.
Fireflies are dragging the hush of evening
                                    up from the damp grass.
Into the world's tumult, into the chaos of every day,
Go quietly, quietly.

THINKING OF DAVID SUMMERS
AT THE BEGINNING OF WINTER

December, five days till Christmas,
                          mercury red-lined
In the low twenties, glass throat
Holding the afternoon half-hindered
And out of luck.
                 Goodbye to my last poem, "Autumn Thoughts."

Two electric wall heaters
                    thermostat on and off,
Ice one-hearted and firm in the mouth of the downspout
Outside, snow stiff as a wedding dress
Carelessly left unkempt
                    all week in another room.

Everything we desire is somewhere else,
                              day too short,
Night too short, light snuffed and then relit,
Road salted and sanded down,
Sky rolling the white of its eye back
                         into its head.

Reinvention is what we're after,
                         Pliny's outline,
Living in history without living in the past
Is what the task is,
Quartering our desire,
                 making what isn't as if it were.

CICADA

All morning I've walked about,
                              opening books and closing books,
Sitting in this chair and that chair,
Steady drip on the skylight,
                              steady hum of regret.
Who listens to anyone?
Across the room, bookcases,
                              across the street, summer trees.

Hear what the book says:
                              This earthly light
Is a seasoning, tempting and sweet and dangerous.
Resist the allurements of the eye.
Feet still caught in the toils of this world's beauty,

                                             resist

The gratifications of the eye.

                    ———

Noon in the early September rain.
A cicada whines,
                    his voice
Starting to drown through the rainy world,
No ripple of wind,
                    no sound but his song of black wings,
No song but the song of his black wings.

Such emptiness at the heart,
                              such emptiness at the heart of being,
Fills us in ways we can't lay claim to,

Ways immense and without names,

                           husk burning like amber

On tree bark, cicada wind-bodied,

Leaves beginning to rustle now

                     in the dark tree of the self.

———

If time is water, appearing and disappearing

In one heliotropic cycle,

               this rain

That sluices as through an hourglass

Outside the window into the gutter and downspout,

Measures our nature

               and moves the body to music.

The book says, however,

                 time is not body's movement

But memory of body's movement.

Time is not water but the memory of water:

We measure what isn't there.

We measure the silence.

              We measure the emptiness.

TENNESSEE LINE

Afternoon overcast the color of water
                                        smoothed by clouds
That whiten where they enter the near end of the sky.
First day of my fifty-fifth year,
Last week of August limp as a frayed rope in the trees,
Yesterday's noise a yellow dust in my shirt pocket
Beneath the toothpick,
                        the .22 bullet and Amitone.

Sounds drift through the haze,
The shadowless orchard, peach leaves dull in the tall grass,
No wind, no bird shudder.
Green boat on the red Rivanna.
                                Rabbit suddenly in place
By the plum tree, then gone in three bounds.
Downshift of truck gears.

                    ————

In 1958, in Monterey, California,
I wrote a journal of over one hundred pages
About the Tennessee line,
About my imagined unhappiness,
                                and how the sun set like a coffin
Into the grey Pacific.
How common it all was.
                        How uncommon I pictured myself.

Memento scrivi, skull-like and word-drunk,
                                one hundred fourteen pages

Of inarticulate self-pity
Looking at landscape and my moral place within it,
The slurry of words inexorable and dark,
The ethical high ground inexorable and dark
I droned from
                    hoping for prescience and a shibboleth . . .

—————

I remember the word and forget the word
                                    although the word
Hovers in flame around me.
Summer hovers in flame around me.
The overcast breaks like a bone above the Blue Ridge.
A loneliness west of solitude
Splinters into the landscape
                    uncomforting as Braille.

We *are* our final vocabulary,
                    and how we use it.
There is no secret contingency.
There's only the rearrangement, the redescription
Of little and mortal things.
There's only this single body, this tiny garment
Gathering the past against itself,
                    making it otherwise.

LOOKING OUTSIDE THE CABIN WINDOW,
I REMEMBER A LINE BY LI PO

The river winds through the wilderness,
Li Po said
                    of another place and another time.
It does so here as well, sliding its cargo of dragon scales
To gutter under the snuff
                    of marsh willow and tamarack.

Mid-morning, Montana high country,
Jack snipe poised on the scarred fence post,
Pond water stilled and smoothed out,
Swallows dog-fighting under the fast-moving storm clouds.

Expectantly empty, green as a pocket, the meadow waits
For the wind to rise and fill it,
                    first with a dark hand
Then with the rain's loose silver
A second time and a third
                    as the day doles out its hours.

Sunlight reloads and ricochets off the window glass.
Behind the cloud scuts,
                    inside the blue aorta of the sky,
The River of Heaven flows
With its barge of stars,
                    waiting for darkness and a place to shine.

We who would see beyond seeing
                    see only language, that burning field.

MID-WINTER SNOWFALL
IN THE PIAZZA DANTE

Verona, late January . . .
                         Outside the caffè,
The snow, like papier-mâché, settles
Its strips all over Dante's bronze body, and holds fast.

Inside, a grappa
In one hand, a double espresso in the other,
I move through the room, slowly,
                         from chessboard to chessboard.

It's Tuesday, tournament night.
Dante's statue, beyond the window, grows larger and whiter
Under the floodlights
                  and serious Alpine snowfall.

In here I understand nothing,
                         not the chess, not the language,
Not even the narrow, pointed shoes the men all wear.
It's 1959. It's ten-thirty at night. I've been in the country for one week.

The nineteenth-century plush
                         on the chairs and loveseats
Resonates, purple and gold.
Three boards are in play in the front room, one in the bar.

My ignorance is immense,
                  as is my happiness.
Caught in the glow of all things golden
And white, I think, at twenty-three, my life has finally begun.

At a side table, under
The tulip-shaped lamps, a small group drinks to a wedding:
"Tutti maschi," the groom toasts,
                    and everyone lifts his full glass.

The huge snowflakes like soft squares
Alternately black and white in the flat light of the piazza,
I vamp in the plush and gold of the mirrors,
                    in love with the world.

That was thirty years ago.
I've learned a couple of things since then
                    not about chess
Or plush or all things golden and white.

Unlike a disease, whatever I've learned
Is not communicable.
                    A singular organism,
It does its work in the dark.

Anything that we think we've learned,
                    we've learned in the dark.
If there is one secret to this life, it is this life.
This life and its hand-me-downs,
                    bishop to pawn 4, void's gambit.

SPRUNG NARRATIVES

What were we thinking of,
                              where were we trying to go,
My brother and I,
That March afternoon almost forty-five years ago,
Up U.S. 11W,
Snow falling, aged ten and eight,
                              so many miles from anyone we knew?

Past Armour Drug, the Civic Auditorium, Brooks Circle
And up the four-lane highway,
Past cornfield and sedgebrush field,
                              past the stone diner and Hillcrest,
Then up the mountain,
Five miles in the late snow,
                              unsure of our whereabouts.

Home, of course, parents abstract with dread,
Three months in a new town,
                              Second World War just over
Some six months before,
                              home to the only home we knew.
Or would know from that day on.
We'd missed the bus. We didn't know what else we should do.

Half-hallowed, half-hand-me-down,
                              our adolescence loomed
At walk's end, eager to gather us.
We let it.
And learned to dance with it, cumbersome, loath, in our arms.

And learned its numbers.

                        And learned its names.

How impossible now to reach it,
No matter how close we come

                        driving by in the car—

That childhood,
That landscape we pictured ourselves a no-cut part of
For good—

            each time we revisit it.

————

Returned to the dwarf orchard,

                    Pilgrim,

Sit still and lengthen your lines,
Shorten your poems and listen to what the darkness says
With its mouthful of cold air.

Midnight, cloud-scatter and cloud-vanish,

                        sky black-chill and black-clear,

South wind through the March-bare trees,
House shadows and hedge shadows.
It's your life. Take it.

            Next month, next year, who knows where you will be.

————

It's Saturday night,

                summer of 1963,

The Teatro Farnese in Rome.
For 150 lire,

            it's Sordi and Gassman
In Mario Monicelli's *La Grande Guerra.*

Alberto Sordi and Vittorio Gassman, World War I
And the north Italian front.
                              Such unwilling heroes!
Sordi a Roman, Gassman a conscript from the Veneto,
Each speaking his dialect,
                    each speaking, to my ears, as though in tongues.

But not to the *romanacci*
                    howling in recognition,
Sending each *stronzo*, each *fijo de na mignota*,
Back at the screen in an ecstasy
Of approval. Who *are* you, it asks?
                    Semmo l'anima de li mortacci tui . . .

Who knows what the story line
                              became, what happened to happen
At movie's end. What's brought back
Is not the occasion but its events,
                              the details
Surrounding it that nicked us.

The world is a language we never quite understand,
But think we catch the drift of.
                              Speaking in ignorance
And joy, we answer
What wasn't asked, by someone we don't know, in strange tongues,

Hoping to get the roll right—
Across the Tiber,
                    past Belli and Dante, off to supper
Scorching the kamikaze Fiats,
A li mortacci tui, brutto zozzo, v'a fa'un culo . . .

———

After it's over, after the last gaze has shut down,
Will I have become
The landscape I've looked at and walked through
Or the road that took me there
                    or the time it took to arrive?

How are we balanced out,
                    by measure, number and weight
As the Renaissance had it,
The idea of God with a compass or gold protractor in his hand?
Lovely to think so,
                    the landscape and journey as one . . .

———

Seventeen years in Laguna Beach—
Month after month the same weather,
                    year after year the same blue
Stretched like a tent-half above our heads.
Even the rain was predictable
When it rounded the Isthmus on Catalina
                    and curtained ashore.

Even the waves seemed laid back
And cool,
                    tweaking the beaches with their tremulous sighs
Of smooth self-satisfaction.
Barely filling the tide pools,
                    languishing back and forth
Between moon-pull and earth-pull.

The walkway unwound along the cliffs
Overlooking all this,
                    and dipped to the pale shoreline
Like an Ace bandage. Down it I went
Each afternoon that I could,
Down to the burning sand,
                    down to the lid of the ocean's great blind eye.

Always the same ghost-figures
Haunting the boardwalk, the basketball courts and the beach.
Always the same shades
                    turning their flat, cocoa-buttered faces
Into the sun-glare,
Pasty, unchangeable faces,
                    unchangeable bodies impatient, unfulfilled.

I walked among them, booted, black-jacketed, peering
Unsurreptitiously into
                    whatever was recognizable.
I never knew anyone.
The sea with its one eye stared. I stared.
For seventeen years we both stared
                    as they turned like blank souls toward the sun.

                    ———

This text is a shadow text.
Under its images, under its darkened prerogatives,
Lie the lines of youth,
                    golden, and lipped in a white light.
They sleep as their shadows move

As though in a dream,
                       disconnected, unwished-upon.
And slightly distorted. And slightly out of control.
Their limbs gleam and their eyelids gleam,
                             under whose soft skin
The little dances and paroxysms leap and turn.

Spot, pivot and spin . . . Spot, pivot and spin . . .
                               Esposito breaks
From the black-robed, black-cordovaned
Body of student priests
                     and feints down the wave-tongued sand
Like a fabulous bird where the tide sifts out and in.

His cassock billows and sighs
As he sings a show tune this morning at Ostia,
Rehearsing the steps and pirouettes
                         he had known by heart once
Last year in another life.

Behind him, like small fists,
                     the others open and close
Around the two German girls
Whose father has laid on and paid for
Their trip to the beach with American priests-to-be

Who drink at his *birreria* on Via della Croce.
                               September, still 1963.
Two months from now, Jerry Jacobson
Will burst through the door
Of my tiny apartment on Via del Babuino

And tell me that President Kennedy has been shot.
Two months.
                    But for now Esposito
Relives his turns and stage days,
The priests remember or reinvent,
                              Maria Luisa

And Astrid pretend
                    their charms will never dissolve or die back
In marriage and motherhood,
And I, the teacher of noun and verb
                    in a language they can't quite understand,
Hum with Esposito and covet their golden hair.

                    _____

Something surrounds us we can't exemplify, something
Mindless and motherless,
                    dark as diction and twice told.
We hear it at night.
Flake by flake,
          we taste it like tinfoil between our teeth.

Under the little runnels of snow,
                              under the mist
settling like moonlight
Over the orchard,
                    under the grasses and black leaves,
In its hush, in its sky width, it takes our breath away.

                    _____

How small it is, and remote,
                    like a photograph from a friend's album

Of the house he lived in as a child.
Or our house seen from next door
Through the bathroom window,

                              a curtain pushed to one side.
How barren the porch looks, how forlorn the rosebushes.

Inside the front room, there are different lights in different places.
Different cars block the driveway.
Where has the tree gone

                        that feathered the summer air with music?
Where is the white throat
That settled the dark, and that darkness settled itself inside?

The valley has been filled in

                        with abandoned structures.
New roads that have been bypassed
By newer roads

                glint in the late sun and disappear.
As twilight sinks in
Across the landscape,

                  lights come on like the lights next door . . .

Seeing the past so

                diminishes it and us too,
Both of us crowding the ghost ramp
And path along the strawberry patch and peanut field,
Down through the hemlocks and apple trees
Behind the house,

                into the black hole of history.

What's left?

            A used leaf shredder, empty begonia pots,

Some memory like a dot
Of light retreating, smaller and sharper with each glance,
Nobody left to remember it
But us,
        half hidden behind a bathroom window curtain? I guess so.

BROKEN ENGLISH

Spring like smoke in the fruit trees,
Ambulance siren falling away
                    through the thick grass.
I gaze at the sky and cut lines from my long poem.

————

What matters we only tell ourselves.

Without the adjective there is no evil or good.

All speech pulls toward privacy
                    and the zones of the infinite.

Better to say what you mean than to mean what you say.

Without a syntax, there is no immortality.

————

Truth's an indefinite article.
When we live, we live for the last time,
                    as Akhmatova says,
One *the* in a world of *a*.

MAPLE ON THE HILL

October again. Faint pheasant tail
Slips through and ruffles the maple tree.

                            A few feathers
Leaf down to cuckold the grass.
Power lines shine, cars shine.

                     Season of glass-glint and edge,

Abracadabra of sunlight,

                cut and spin.
The day saws itself in half.
Northwest wind has something up its sleeve.
At the horned heart of the labyrinth,

                      the unsayable has its say.

Don't forget me, little darling, when they've laid me down to die.
Just one little wish, darling, that I pray.
As you linger there in sadness you are thinking of the past,
Let your teardrops kiss the flowers on my grave.

The mirror of history swallows its images:
It never repeats itself

               in us, its distorted children.
Each life, as Plutarch tells us,
Contains many lives,

            some recognizable, some not.

History's just another story.
In the City of the Dead, no one
                  stands up and says, *Here I am, I'm your boy.*
Discontinuous, discrete,
The hunter, history's dog, will sniff us,
                                    sure as hell . . .

CHICKAMAUGA

Dove-twirl in the tall grass.
　　　　　　　　　End-of-summer glaze next door
On the gloves and split ends of the conked magnolia tree.
Work sounds: truck back-up-beep, wood tin-hammer, cicada, fire horn.

―――――

History handles our past like spoiled fruit.
Mid-morning, late-century light
　　　　　　　　　calicoed under the peach trees.
Fingers us here. Fingers us here and here.

―――――

The poem is a code with no message:
The point of the mask is not the mask but the face underneath,
Absolute, incommunicado,
　　　　　　　　　unhoused and peregrine.

―――――

The gill net of history will pluck us soon enough
From the cold waters of self-contentment we drift in
One by one
　　　　　　　　　into its suffocating light and air.

―――――

Structure becomes an element of belief, syntax
And grammar a catechist,
Their words what the beads say,
　　　　　　　　　words thumbed to our discontent.

STILL LIFE ON A MATCHBOX LID

The heart is colder than the eye is.
The watchers, the holy ones,
                    know this, no shortcut to the sky.
A single dog hair can split the wind.

If you want great tranquility,
                    it's hard work and a long walk.
Don't brood on the past.
The word is without appendages,
                    no message, no name.

BLAISE PASCAL LIP-SYNCS THE VOID

It's not good to be complete.
It's not good to be concupiscent,
     caught as we are
Between a the and a the,
Neither of which we know and neither of which knows us.
It's not good to be sewn shut.

There's change and succession in all things, Pascal contends,
But inconstancy, boredom and anxiety condition our days.
Neither will wash for him, though,
      since nature is corrupt.
That's why we love it.
    That's why we take it, unwinnowed,
Willingly into our hearts.

December. 4 p.m.
    Chardonnay-colored light-slant
Lug weight in the boned trees.
      Squirrel dead on the Tarmac.
Boom-boxing Big Foot pickup trucks
Hustle down Locust,
    light pomegranate pink grapefruit then blood.
We take it into our hearts.

WINTER-WORSHIP

Mother of Darkness, Our Lady,
Suffer our supplications,
                              our hurts come unto you.
Hear us from absence your dwelling place,
Whose ear we plead for.
                              End us our outstay.

Where darkness is light, what can the dark be,
                                        whose eye is single,
Whose body is filled with splendor
In winter,
                    inside the snowflake, inside the crystal of ice
Hung like Jerusalem from the tree.

January, rain-wind and sleet-wind,
Snow pimpled and pock-marked,
                                    half slush-hearted, half brocade,
Under your noon-dimmed day watch,
Whose alcove we harbor in,
                              whose waters are beaded and cold.

A journey's a fragment of Hell,
                              one inch or a thousand miles.
Darken our disbelief, dog our steps.
Inset our eyesight,
Radiance, loom and sting,
                              whose ashes rise from the flames.

THE SILENT GENERATION

Afternoons in the backyard, our lives like photographs
Yellowing elsewhere,
                            in somebody else's album,
In secret, January south winds
Ungathering easily through the black limbs of the fruit trees.

What was it we never had to say?
                            Who can remember now—
Something about the world's wrongs,
Something about the way we shuddered them off like rain
In an open field,
                            convinced that lightning would not strike.

We're arm in arm with regret, now left foot, now right foot.
We give the devil his due.
We walk up and down in the earth,
                            we take our flesh in our teeth.
When we die, we die. The wind blows away our footprints.

AN ORDINARY AFTERNOON
IN CHARLOTTESVILLE

Under the peach trees, the ideograms the leaves throw
Over the sun-prepped grass read
Purgatio, illuminatio, contemplatio,
Words caught in a sweet light endurable,

        unlike the one they lead to,
Whose sight we're foundered and fallowed by.

Meanwhile, the afternoon

      fidgets about its business,
Unconcerned with such immolations,
Sprinkle of holy grit from the sun's wheel,

        birds combustible
In the thin leaves incendiary—
Fire, we think, marvellous fire, everything starts in fire.

Or so they say. We like to think so
Ourselves, feeling the cold

      glacier into the blood stream
A bit more each year,
Tasting the iron disk on our tongues,
Watching the birds oblivious,

     hearing their wise chant, *hold still, hold still . . .*

MONDO ANGELICO

Fish never sleep.
                Aquatic angels,
They drift in the deep ether of all their rectitude,
Half dark, half flicker of light
At the eye's edge,
                    their shadows shadows of shadows—

Under the blue spruce,
Under the skunkweed and onion head,
Under the stump,
                  the aspergillum of the dew-rose,
They signal and disappear.

Like lost thoughts,
                  they wouldn't remember us if they could,
Hovering just out of touch,
Their bodies liminal, their sights sealed.
Always they disregard us
                with a dull disregard.

MONDO HENBANE

The journey ends between the black spiders and the white spiders,
As Blake reminds us.
                              For now,
However, pain is the one thing that fails to actualize
Where the green-backed tree swallows dip
                                        and the wood ducks glide

Over the lodgepole's soft slash.
Little islands of lime-green pine scum
Float on the pot-pond water.
                              Load-heavy bumblebees
Lower themselves to the sun-swollen lupine and paintbrush throats.

In the front yard, a half mile away,
                              one robin stretches his neck out,
Head cocked to the ground,
Hearing the worm's hum or the worm's heart.
Or hearing the spiders fly,
                  on their fiery tracks, through the smoke-choked sky.

MILES DAVIS AND ELIZABETH BISHOP
FAKE THE BREAK

Those two dark syllables, *begin*,
                                        offer no sustenance,
Nor does this pale squish of September sunlight unwound
Across the crabgrass.

The silence is cold, like an instrument in the hand
Which cannot be set aside,
Unlike our suffering, so easy, so difficult.

Still, the warmth on our skin is nice,
                                        and the neighbor's pears,
Late pears, dangle like golden hourglasses above our heads.

"It's just description," she said,
                                        "they're all just description."
Meaning her poems . . . Mine, too,
The walleye of morning's glare
                                        lancing the landscape,
The dogwood berries as red as cinnamon drops in the trees,
Sunday, the twenty-ninth of September, 1991.

From the top . . . Beginning in ignorance, we stick to the melody—
Knowledge, however, is elsewhere,
                                        a tune we've yet to turn to,
Its syllables scrubbed in light, its vestibules empty.

PECCATOLOGY

As Kafka has told us,
                    sin always comes openly:
It walks on its roots and doesn't have to be torn out.

How easily it absolves itself in the senses,
However, in Indian summer,
                                the hedge ivy's star-feet
Treading the dead spruce and hemlock spurs,
The last leaves like live coals
                    banked in the far corners of the yard,
The locust pods in Arabic letters, right to left.

How small a thing it becomes, nerve-sprung
And half electric,
                    deracinated, full of joy.

EAST OF THE BLUE RIDGE,
OUR TOMBS ARE IN THE DOVE'S THROAT

Late Sunday in Charlottesville.
We cross our arms like effigies, look up at the sky
And wait for a sign of salvation—
                              as Lorca has taught us to say,
Two and two never make four down here,
They always make two and two.

Five crows roust a yellow-tailed hawk from the hemlock tree next door,
Black blood spots dipping and blown
Across the relentless leeching
                    the sun pales out of the blue.

We'd like to fly away ourselves, pushed
Or pulled, into or out of our own bodies,
                              into or out of the sky's mouth.
We'd like to disappear into a windfall of light.

But the numbers don't add up.
Besides, a piece of jar glass
                    burns like a star at the street's edge,
The elbows and knuckled limb joints of winter trees,
Shellacked by the sunset, flash and fuse,
Windows blaze
          and the earthly splendor roots our names to the ground.

"NOT EVERYONE CAN SEE THE TRUTH, BUT HE CAN BE IT"

Sunday. It's always Sunday.

                                   Rifts and seams of dark birds
Right-flank and wheel across a darker December sky
Southwest and so wide.

Winter solstice again,

                         burnt end of a narrow road.
The lawn chairs gutter and glare in their white solitude.

How short the days are.

How imperceptibly we become ourselves—

                             like solstice-diminishing light
Devolving to one appointed spot,
We substitute and redress
In predetermined degrees we've neither a heart nor hand in.

How slowly the streetlights come on.

                             How shrill the birds are.

Take off your traveling clothes and

                         lay down your luggage,
Pilgrim, shed your nakedness.
Only the fire is absorbed by the Holy of Holies.

                                Let it shine.

AS OUR BODIES RISE,
OUR NAMES TURN INTO LIGHT

The sky unrolls like a rug,
                              unwelcoming, gun-grey,
Over the Blue Ridge.
Mothers are calling their children in,
                              mellifluous syllables, floating sounds.
The traffic shimmies and settles back.

The doctor has filled his truck with leaves
Next door, and a pair of logs.
                              Salt stones litter the street.
The snow falls and the wind drops.
How strange to have a name, any name, on this poor earth.

January hunkers down,
                              the icicle deep in her throat—
The days become longer, the nights ground bitter and cold,
Single grain by single grain
Everything flows toward structure,
                              last ache in the ache for God.

ABSENCE INSIDE AN ABSENCE

We live in the world of the voice,
                       not in the world of the word,
According to John the Solitary—
Our lives are language, our desires are apophatic,
The bush in flame is the bush in flame,
Imageless heart, imageless absence between the hearts.

And if we cry out,
                  if once we utter our natural sounds,
Even the angels will hide their heads
Under their blue wings,
                    it's also said.
So better forget that, better forget the darkness above the tongue,
Its shorting of words, its mad silence and lack of breath.

Besides, there's another spin,
The flame and counterflame by which we come to stillness
Playing over our faces,
                   over the rose cane and the missing rose,
Over the dreary schooners of snow
Pulling their nets in across the yard,
                    over their waters brought to joy.

Still, the idea of absence inside an absence
Completing a presence is dynamite,
                   the showings foretold
Unseeable through the earthly eye,
We say to ourselves,
The earth in our cracked hands,
                  the earth dark syllables in our mouths.

STILL LIFE WITH SPRING
AND TIME TO BURN

Warm day, early March. The buds preen, busting their shirtwaists
All over the plum trees. Blue moan of the mourning dove.
It's that time again,
                                    time of relief, time of sorrow
The earth is afflicted by.
We feel it ourselves, a bright uncertainty of what's to come

Swelling our own skins with sweet renewal, a kind of disease
That holds our affections dear
                                    and asks us to love it.
And so we do, supposing
That time and affection is all we need answer to.
But we guess wrong:

Time will append us like suit coats left out overnight
On a deck chair, loose change dead weight in the right pocket,
Silk handkerchief limp with dew,
                                    sleeves in a slow dance with the wind.
And love will kill us—
Love, and the winds from under the earth
                                    that grind us to grain-out.

WITH SIMIC AND MARINETTI
AT THE GIUBBE ROSSE

Where Dino Campana once tried to sell his sad poems
Among the tables,
Where Montale settled into his silence and hid,
Disguised as himself for twenty years,
The ghosts of Papini and Prezzolini sit tight
With Carlo Emilio Gadda
                              somewhere behind our backs.

Let's murder the moonlight, let's go down
On all fours and mewl like the animals and make it mean what it means.
Not even a stir.
Not even a breath across the plates of *gnocchi* and roast veal.
Like everything else in Florence, that's part of the past,
The wind working away away kneading the sea so muscles . . .

Those who don't remember the Futurists are condemned to repeat
      them.
We order a grappa. We order a mineral water.
Little by little, the lucid, warm smile of the moon
Overflowed from the torn clouds.
                              Some ran.
A cry was heard in the solitude of the high plains.
Simic e Wright sulla traccia. La luna ammazzata.

TO THE EGYPTIAN MUMMY IN
THE ETRUSCAN MUSEUM AT CORTONA

Wrapped like a sprained ankle from head to toe,
                                        locked in glass
In an inconceivable country,
Spun on the sprung reflections caught in a stranger's eye
Year after year,
                you would not imagine yourself if you could,
Peninsulaed as you are, and rare.

Outside the window, sun rains on the Middle Ages.
An upupa pecks in the tall grass.
Under the stone walls and stone towers,
                                the hillside unravels its tapestry,
A picnic in spring's green fire: one man's asleep and a young girl
Claps time for her brother who hand-dances with his dog.

One half-expects, say, Guidoriccio da Fogliano
In full regalia,
Or Malatesta, at least, at large from the Marches,
To climb the gut-twisted road through the quicksilver glint and tufa
    stone
Toward the south gate and you,
                pale messenger from the wordless world . . .

Leonardo, Vasari says,
                would purchase the caged, white doves
As he walked through the market sprawl of San Lorenzo
In order to set them free. I'll do

The same thing for you, unlatching this landscape, the vine rows and
  olive trees,
Till its wingspread shrinks to a radiance.

                              Look. Already it's getting smaller.

WITH EDDIE AND NANCY IN AREZZO
AT THE CAFFÈ GRANDE

Piero in wraps, the True Cross *sotto restauro*,
Piazza desolate edge
Where sunlight breaks it,
                              desolate edge
Where sunlight pries it apart.
A child kicks a soccer ball. Another heads it back.

The Fleeting World, Po Chü-i says, short-hops a long dream,
No matter if one is young or old—
The pain of what is present never comes to an end,
Lightline moving inexorably
West to east across the stones,
                              cutting the children first, then cutting us.

Under the archways, back and forth among the tables,
The blind ticket seller taps and slides.
Lotteria di Foligno, Lotteria di Foligno,
                              he intones,
Saturday, mid-May, cloud bolls high cotton in the Tuscan sky.
One life is all we're entitled to, but it's enough.

THERE IS NO SHELTER

Each evening, the sins of the whole world collect here like a dew.
In the morning, little galaxies, they flash out
And flame,
                    their charred, invisible residue etching

The edges our lives take and the course of things, filling
The shadows in,
                    an aftertrace, through the discards of the broken world,
Like the long, slow burn of a struck match.

WATCHING THE EQUINOX ARRIVE
IN CHARLOTTESVILLE, SEPTEMBER 1992

2:23 p.m.
                The season glides to a click.
Nobody says a word
From where I sit, shadows dark flags from nothing's country,
Birds in the deep sky, then not,
Cricket caught in the outback between a grass spear and a leaf.
The quince bush
Is losing its leaves in the fall's early chemotherapy,
And stick-stemmed spikes of the lemon tree
Spink in the sun.
Autumnal outtakes, autumnal stills . . .

Mockingbird, sing me a song.
Back here, where the windfall apples rot to the bee's joy,
Where the peach sheaths and pear sheaths piebald and brindle,
Where each year the orchard unlearns
                                everything it's been taught,
The weekend's rainfall
Pools its untroubled waters,
Doves putter about in the still-green limbs of the trees,
Ants inch up the cinder blocks and lawn spiders swing from the vines.
You've got to learn to unlearn things, the season repeats.
For every change there's a form.

———

Open your mouth, you are lost, close your mouth, you are lost,
So the Buddhists say.
                They also say,
Live in the world unattached to the dust of the world.

Not so easy to do when the thin, monotonous tick of the universe
Painfully pries our lips apart,
                              and dirties our tongues
With soiled, incessant music.
Not so easy to do when the right front tire blows out,
Or the phone rings at 3 a.m.
                    and the ghost-voice says, "It's 911, please hold."
They say, enter the blackness, the form of forms. They say,
No matter how we see ourselves, sleeping and dreaming see us as light.

Still, there's another story,
                    that what's inside us is what's outside us:
That what we see outside ourselves we'll soon see inside ourselves.
It's visible, and is our garment.
Better, perhaps, to wear that.
Better to live as though we already lived the afterlife,
Unattached to our cape of starred flesh.
But Jesus said,
            Lift up the stone and you will find me,
Break open a piece of wood, I'm there.
It's hard to argue with that,
Hard to imagine a paradise beyond what the hand breaks.

———————

For every force there's a change.
Mouthful of silence, mouthful of air,
                              sing me your tune.
The wind leaves nothing alone.
How many times can summer turn to fall in one life?
Well you might ask, my old friend,
Wind-rider, wind-spirit, seeking my blood out,
                              humming my name.

Hard work, this business of solitude.
Hard work and no gain,
Mouthful of silence, mouthful of air.
Everything's more than it seems back here. Everything's less.

Like migrating birds, our own lives drift away from us.
How small they become in the blank sky, how colorful,
On their way to wherever they please.
We keep our eyes on the ground,
                                    on the wasp and pinch bug,
As the years grind by and the seasons churn, north and south.
We keep our eyes on the dirt.
Under the limp fins of the lemon tree, we inhabit our absence.
Crows cross-hatch and settle in,
                                    red birds and dust sparrows
Spindle and dart through the undergrowth.
We don't move. We watch, but we don't move.

WAITING FOR TU FU

Snip, snip goes wind through the autumn trees.
I move my bed to the battlefront,
                        dead leaves like a blanket of moth bodies
Up to the necks of the cold grasses.
It crunches like pecan shells underfoot.
It crinks my back where I lie
                        gazing into the beaten artifice
Of gold leaf and sky.

How vast the clouds are, how vast as they troll and pass by.
Splendid and once-removed, like lives, they never come back.
Does anyone think of them?
Everything's golden from where I lie.
                                Even the void
Beyond the void the clouds cross.
Even the knowledge that everything's fire,
                        and nothing ever comes back.

All that was yesterday, or last week,
Or somebody else's line of talk.
                        Words rise like mist from my body,
Prayer-smoke, a snowy comfort.
The Greek-thin hammered gold artifacts
                        and glazed inlay
Of landscape and sky
Accept it as incense, for they are used to such things.

———

What have you done with your life,
                        you've asked me, as you've asked yourself,

What has it come to,
Carrying us like a barge toward the century's end
And sheer drop-off into millennial history?
I remember an organ chord one Sunday in North Carolina.
I remember the smell of white pines,

                            Vitalis and lye soap.

O we were pure and holy in those days,
The August sunlight candescing our short-sleeved shirt fronts,
The music making us otherwise.
O we were abstract and true.
How could we know that grace would fall from us like shed skin,
That reality, our piebald dog, would hunt us down?

The seasons reshuffle and set me.
Cattle as large as clouds

                        lumber across my mind's sky
And children rise in the wind
Like angels over the lake, sad cataracted eye—

I remember cutting its surface once in a green canoe,
Eye that saw everything, that now sees nothing at all . . .

                   ————

Where is my life going in these isolate outlands,
You questioned once in a verse.
I ask the same thing,

                      wreckage of broken clouds too far to count,
The landscape, like God, a circle whose center is everywhere
And circumference nowhere,
Dead end of autumn, everything caught between stone-drift and
    stone.

Black winter bird flocks side-wheel
From tree lung to grief-empty tree lung,
                              lawn furniture
Imprints, unsat in. It's late.
Darkness, black phosphorus, smokes forth in the peaches and white pines.
The pile driver footing the new bridge
Cuts off, the bird flocks cough up and out.

I've read *Reflections in Autumn*,
            I've been through the Three Gorges, I've done Chengdu . . .
Much easier here to find you out,
A landscape yourself by now,
Canebrake and waterbrake, inviolable in the memory.
Immortals, you once said, set forth again in their boats.
White hair, white hair. Drift away.

PAESAGGIO NOTTURNO

Full moon, the eighth of March; clouds
Cull and disperse; dog's bark, moon
Tracking stage left to stage right;
Maple ganglia, Munch sky.

Small night that pulls me inside,
Fingerless, fatherless; night
Crystalline, sleep-shaped and sharp,
The bulb tufts odd teeth; nightmouth.

All things are found in all things,
Wind in the peach trees, time's dust:
It's in light that light exists.
All flesh, at last, comes to you.

STILL LIFE WITH STICK AND WORD

April is over. May moon.
How many more for my regard,
                              hundreds, a handful?
Better not trouble the dark water due north of north.
Better to concentrate on something close, something small.
This stick, for instance. This word.

Next week. Back in the same chair.
And here's the stick
                    right where I dropped it, deep in the grass.
Maple, most likely, fuzz-barked and twice-broken, spore-pocked
With white spots, star charts to ford the river of heaven.
Warm wood. Warm wind from the clouds.

Inside now. The word is *white*.
It covers my tongue like paint—
                                I say it and light forms,
Bottles arise, emptiness opens its corridors
Into the entrances and endless things that form bears.
White, great eviscerator.

Out into absence. Night chair.
Rose constellations rise
                        up from the shed and sad trees,
White yips in the dog dark that mirror the overburn.
A slide of houselight escapes through the kitchen window.
How unlike it is. How like.

SUMMER STORM

As Mondrian knew,
Art is the image of an image of an image,
More vacant, more transparent
With each repeat and slough:
                      one skin, two skins, it comes clear,
An old idea not that old.

Two rectangles, red and grey, from 1935,
Distant thunder like distant thunder—
Howitzer shells, large
                  dropoffs into drumbeat and roll.
And there's that maple again,
Head like an African Ice Age queen, full-leafed and lipped.

Behind her, like clear weather,
Mondrian's window gives out
                    onto ontology,
A dab of red, a dab of grey, white interstices.
You can't see the same thing twice,
As Mondrian knew.

LOOKING WEST FROM LAGUNA BEACH
AT NIGHT

I've always liked the view from my mother-in-law's house at night,
Oil rigs off Long Beach
Like floating lanterns out in the smog-dark Pacific,
Stars in the eucalyptus,
Lights of airplanes arriving from Asia, and town lights
Littered like broken glass around the bay and back up the hill.

In summer, dance music is borne up
On the sea winds from the hotel's beach deck far below,
"Twist and Shout," or "Begin the Beguine."
It's nice to think that somewhere someone is having a good time,
And pleasant to picture them down there
Turned out, tipsy and flushed, in their white shorts and their turquoise
    shirts.

Later, I like to sit and look up
At the mythic history of Western civilization,
Pinpricked and clued through the zodiac.
I'd like to be able to name them, say what's what and how who got
    where,
Curry the physics of metamorphosis and its endgame,
But I've spent my life knowing nothing.

LOOKING AGAIN AT WHAT I LOOKED AT
FOR SEVENTEEN YEARS

Quick pink; Soutine meat-streaks in the west,
Ocean grey drop cloth underfoot;
                              peroxided gums—
Memory's like that, mixed metaphors, time's drone and gouache
Hovering near the horizon, black
Instinct filling the edges in, resplendent with holes.

We have it for text and narrative—
                              nothing is new,
Remembrance, both nerve-net and nerve-spring,
The connection of everything with everything else
(Like absences the sea fills),
Constructs us and deconstructs us, world's breath, world's body.

Down there, for instance, just past the security lights
The hotel fans, wave-hollows build and dispense, surf sighs
And the unseen undertow
Sucks it away to where it's unreachable for good
Until it all comes back . . .
                              It's like that.

LOOKING ACROSS LAGUNA CANYON
AT DUSK, WEST-BY-NORTHWEST

I love the way the evening sun goes down,
                              orange brass-plaque, life's loss-logo,
Behind the Laguna hills and bare night-wisps of fog.
I love the way the hills empurple and sky goes nectarine,
The way the lights appear like little electric fig seeds, the wet west
Burnishing over into the indeterminate colors of the divine.

Like others, I want to pour myself into the veins of the invisible
at times like this,
                        becoming all that's liquid and moist.
Like Dionysus, I'd enter the atmosphere, spread and abandon—
They'd have to look for me elsewhere then,
Trickle of light extinguished in the Pacific, dark sluice, dark sluice line.

VENEXIA I

Too much at first, too lavish—full moon
Jackhammering light-splints along the canal, gondola beaks
Blading the half-dark;
Moon-spar; backwash backlit with moon-spark . . .

Next morning, all's otherwise
With a slow, chill rainfall like ragweed
                              electric against the launch lights,
Then grim-grained, then grey.
This is the water-watch landscape, the auto-da-fé.

Such small atrocities these days between the columns,
Such pale seductions and ravishments.
Boats slosh on the crushed canal, gulls hunch down, the weather rubs
        us away.
From here it's a long walk home.

Listen, Venice is death by drowning, everyone knows,
City of masks and minor frightfulness, October city
Twice sunk in its own sad skin.
How silently the lagoon
                        covers our footsteps, how quickly.

Along the Zattere, the liners drift huge as clouds.
We husband our imperfections, our changes of tune.
When water comes for us, we take it into our arms—
What's left's affection, and that's our sin.

VENEXIA II

Acqua alta, high water,
                                         sea gull anchored like Rimbaud's boat
Among the detritus, stuffed plastic food sacks bobbing like corks
Under Our Lady's stone-stern gaze,
                                         Veneẓia, Serenissima . . .
Tide-slosh nibbles our shoe tops, then stumbles them under.

These are the dark waters, dark music
That scours us, that empties us out
                                         only to fill us back by inches
With sweet, invisible plentitude,
Notes of astonishment, black notes to leave our lives by.

The Angel of Death, with her golden horn and her golden robe,
Rocks on the gondola's prow,
                                         rain-dazzled, lashed at ease.
Under the rainfall's doom date,
She shines in her maritime solitude, she slides in splendor.

Outside the window, Rio San Polo churns and squalls.
The *traghetto*'s light
Burns like a homing Cathar soul
                                         over the slack tide
Descending the greened Salute's steps.

This is the terminate hour, its bell
Tumbling out of Santa Maria Gloriosa dei Frari,
Last link in the chain of Speculation,
                                         pulling us under.
Water is what it comes from, water is where it goes.

YARD WORK

I think that someone will remember us in another time,
Sappho once said—more or less—
Her words caught
Between the tongue's tip and the first edge of the invisible.

I hope so, myself now caught
Between the edge of the landscape and the absolute,
Which is the same place, and the same sound,
That she made.

Meanwhile, let's stick to business.
Everything else does, the landscape, the absolute, the invisible.
My job is yard work—
I take this inchworm, for instance, and move it from here to there.

BLACK ZODIAC

APOLOGIA PRO VITA SUA

I

How soon we come to road's end—
Failure, our two-dimensional side-kick, flat dream-light,
Won't jump-start or burn us in,

Dogwood insidious in its constellations of part-charred cross points,
Spring's via Dolorosa
                    flashed out in a dread profusion,
Nowhere to go but up, nowhere to turn, dead world-weight,

They've gone and done it again,
                dogwood,
Spring's sap-crippled, arthritic, winter-weathered, myth limb,
Whose roots are my mother's hair.

Landscape's a lever of transcendence—
                    jack-wedge it here,
Or here, and step back,
Heave, and a light, a little light, will nimbus your going forth:

The dew bead, terminal bead, opens out
                    onto a great radiance,
Sun's square on magnolia leaf
Offers us entrance—
          who among us will step forward,

Camellia brown boutonnieres
Under his feet, plum branches under his feet, white sky, white
    noon,
Church bells like monk's mouths tonguing the hymn?

————————

Journal and landscape
—Discredited form, discredited subject matter—
I tried to resuscitate both, breath and blood,
                          making them whole again

Through language, strict attention—
Verona mi fe', disfecemi Verona, the song goes.
I've hummed it, I've bridged the break

To no avail.
         April. The year begins beyond words,
Beyond myself and the image of myself, beyond
Moon's ice and summer's thunder. All that.

————————

The meat of the sacrament is invisible meat and a ghostly substance.
I'll say.
        Like any visible thing,
I'm always attracted downward, and soon to be killed and assimilated.

Vessel of life, it's said, vessel of life, brought to naught,
Then gathered back to what's visible.
That's it, fragrance of spring like lust in the blossom-starred orchard,

The shapeless shape of darkness starting to seep through and emerge,
The seen world starting to tilt,

Where I sit the still, unwavering point
                            under that world's waves.

―――――――

How like the past the clouds are,
Building and disappearing along the horizon,
Inflecting the mountains,
                    laying their shadows under our feet

For us to cross over on.
Out of their insides fire falls, ice falls,
What we remember that still remembers us, earth and air fall.

Neither, however, can resurrect or redeem us,
Moving, as both must, ever away toward opposite corners.
Neither has been where we're going,
                            bereft of an attitude.

―――――――

Amethyst, crystal transparency,
                        Maya and Pharaoh ring,
Malocchio, set against witchcraft,
Lightning and hailstorm, birthstone, savior from drunkenness.

Purple, color of insight, clear sight,
Color of memory—
                    violet, that's for remembering,
Star-crystals scattered across the penumbra, hard stars.

Who can distinguish darkness from the dark, light from light,
Subject matter from story line,
                        the part from the whole
When whole is part of the part and part is all of it?

73

Lonesomeness. Morandi, Cézanne, it's all about lonesomeness.
And Rothko. Especially Rothko.
Separation from what heals us

                    beyond painting, beyond art.

Words and paint, black notes, white notes.
Music and landscape; music, landscape and sentences.
Gestures for which there is no balm, no intercession.

Two tone fields, horizon a line between abysses,
Generally white, always speechless.
Rothko could choose either one to disappear into. And did.

Perch'io no spero di tornar giammai, ballatetta, in Toscana,
Not as we were the first time,

                    not as we'll ever be again.
Such snowflakes of memory, they fall nowhere but there.

Absorbed in remembering, we cannot remember—
Exile's anthem, O stiff heart,
Thingless we came into the world and thingless we leave.

Every important act is wordless—

                    to slip from the right way,
To fail, still accomplishes something.
Even a good thing remembered, however, is not as good as not
    remembering at all.

Time is the source of all good,

                  time the engenderer

Of entropy and decay.
Time the destroyer, our only-begetter and advocate.

For instance, my fingernail,
                              so pink, so amplified,
In the half-dark, for instance,
These force-fed dogwood blossoms, green-leafed, defused,
                              limp on their long branches.

St. Stone, say a little prayer for me,
                              grackles and jay in the black gum,
Drowse of the peony head,
Dandelion globes luminous in the last light, more work to be done . . .

II

Something will get you, the doctor said,

                                don't worry about that.

Melancholia's got me,

Pains in the abdomen, pains down the left leg and crotch.

Slurry of coal dust behind the eyes,

Massive weight in the musculature, dark blood, dark blood.

I'm sick and tired of my own complaints,

This quick flick like a compass foot through the testicle,

Deep drag and hurt through the groin—

Melancholia, black dog,

                           everyone's had enough.

———

Dew-dangled, fresh-cut lawn grass will always smell like a golf course

Fairway to me, Saturday morning, Chuck Ross and I

Already fudging our scores down,

                      happy as mockingbirds in deep weeds,

The South Fork of the Holston River

Slick as a nickel before its confluence behind our backs

At Rotherwood with the North Fork's distant, blurred thunder,

Our rounds in the seventies always including mulligans,

Nudged lies, "found" lost balls, some extraordinary shots

And that never-again-to-be-repeated

                      teen-age false sense of attainment.

———

One summer, aged 16, I watched—each night, it seemed—my
    roommate,
A college guy, gather his blanket up, and flashlight,
And leave for his rendezvous with the camp cook—
                                    he never came back before dawn.

Some 40 years later I saw him again for the first time
Since then, in a grocery store, in the checkout line,
A cleric from Lexington, shrunken and small. Bearded even.

And all these years I'd thought of him, if at all, as huge
And encompassing,
Not rabbit-eyed, not fumbling a half-filled brown sack,
                                    dry-lipped, apologetic.

                    ———————

In 1990 we dragged Paris
                    —back on the gut again after 25 years—
The Boulevard Montparnasse,
La Coupole, the Select, you know, the Dôme, the Closerie de Lilas,

Up and down and back and forth.
Each night a Japanese girl would take a bath at 4 a.m.
In the room above ours,
                    each night someone beat his wife

In a room above the garage outside our window.
It rained all day for ten days.
Sleeplessness, hallucination, O City of Light . . .

                    ———————

What sane, impossible reason could Percy Heath have made up
To talk to me, drunk, white and awe-struck,

—And tone-deaf to boot—
                    that night at the Carmel Mission?

But talk he did, uncondescending, feigning interest,
As Milt Jackson walked by and John Lewis walked by,
                                        Gerry Mulligan
Slouched in one corner, Paul Desmond cool in an opposite one.

October, 1958, Monterey Jazz Festival,
First advisors starting to leave the Army Language School for
     South Vietnam,
The Pacific's dark eyelid
                    beginning to stir, ready to rise and roll back . . .

———

During World War II, we lived in Oak Ridge, Tennessee,
Badges and gates, checkpoints, government housing, government rules.
One house we lived in was next door to a two-star admiral.

I learned a couple of things in the three-plus years we lived in
     Oak Ridge,
One from my first (and only) paper route, the second
After my first (and only) breaking-and-entering.

One thing I learned, however, I didn't know what to do with:
Death is into the water, life is the coming out.
I still don't, though nothing else matters but that, it seems,
                                nothing even comes close.

———

Elm Grove, Pine Valley and Cedar Hill,
                    what detritus one remembers—

The one-armed soldier we spied on making out in the sedge grass
With his red-haired girl friend behind the Elm Grove playground,

For instance, in 1944 . . . I was nine, the fourth grade . . .
I remember telling Brooklyn, my best friend,
                                    my dick was stiff all night.
Nine years old! My dick! All night!

We talked about it for days,
                        Oak Ridge abstracted and elsewhere,
—D-Day and Normandy come and gone—
All eyes on the new world's sun king,
                                its rising up and its going down.

                    ————

It's Wednesday afternoon, and Carter and I are on the road
For the Sullivan County National Bank Loan Department,
1957, Gate City and Southwest Virginia.

We're after deadbeats, delinquent note payers, in Carter's words.
Cemetery plots—ten dollars a month until you die or pay up.
In four months I'll enter the Army, right now I'm Dr. Death,

Riding shotgun for Carter, bringing more misery to the miserable.
Up-hollow and down-creek, shack after unelectrified shack—
The worst job in the world, and we're the two worst people in it.

                    ————

Overcast afternoon, then weak sun, then overcast again.
A little wind
                whiffles across the back yard like a squall line
In miniature, thumping the clover heads, startling the grass.

My parents' 60th wedding anniversary
Were they still alive,
                    5th of June, 1994.
It's hard to imagine, I think, your own children grown older than you
    ever were, I can't.

I sit in one of the knock-off Brown-Jordan deck chairs we brought
    from California,
Next to the bearded grandson my mother never saw.
Some afternoon, or noon, it will all be over. Not this one.

III

June is a migraine above the eyes,
Strict auras and yellow blots,
                              green screen and tunnel vision,
Slow ripples of otherworldliness,

Humidity's painfall drop by drop.
Next door, high whine of the pest exterminator's blunt machine.
Down the street, tide-slap of hammer-and-nail,
                              hammer-and-nail from a neighbor's roof.

I've had these for forty years,
                              light-prints and shifting screed,
Feckless illuminations.
St. John of the Cross, Julian of Norwich, lead me home.

———

It's good to know certain things:
What's departed, in order to know what's left to come;
That water's immeasurable and incomprehensible

And blows in the air
Where all that's fallen and silent becomes invisible;
That fire's the light our names are carved in.

That shame is a garment of sorrow;
That time is the Adversary, and stays sleepless and wants for nothing;
That clouds are unequal and words are.

I sense a certain uncertainty in the pine trees,
Seasonal discontent,
                                quotidian surliness,
Pre-solstice jitters, that threatens to rattle our equilibrium.

My friend has lost his larynx,
My friend who in the old days, with a sentence or two,
Would easily set things right,

His glasses light-blanks as he quoted a stanza from Stevens or Yeats
Behind his cigarette smoke.
Life's hard, our mutual third friend says . . . It is. It is.

————

Sundays define me.
                                Born on a back-lit Sunday, like today,
But later, in August,
And elsewhere, in Tennessee, Sundays dismantle me.

There is a solitude about Sunday afternoons
In small towns, surrounded by all that's familiar
And of necessity dear,

That chills us on hot days, like today, unto the grave,
When the sun is a tongued wafer behind the clouds, out of sight,
And wind chords work through the loose-roofed yard sheds,
                                                a celestial music . . .

————

There is forgetfulness in me which makes me descend
Into a great ignorance,
And makes me to walk in mud, though what I remember remains.

Some of the things I have forgotten:
Who the Illuminator is, and what he illuminates;
Who will have pity on what needs have pity on it.

What I remember redeems me,
                              strips me and brings me to rest,
An end to what has begun,
A beginning to what is about to be ended.

———————

What are the determining moments of our lives?
                                    How do we know them?
Are they ends of things or beginnings?
Are we more or less of ourselves once they've come and gone?

I think this is one of mine tonight,
The Turkish moon and its one star
                              crisp as a new flag
Over my hometown street with its dark trash cans looming along
    the curb.

Surely this must be one. And what of me afterwards
When the moon and her sanguine consort
Have slipped the horizon? What will become of me then?

———————

Some names are everywhere—they are above and they are below,
They are concealed and they are revealed.
We call them wise, for the wisdom of death is called the little wisdom.

And my name? And your name?
                        Where will we find them, in what pocket?

Wherever it is, better to keep them there not known—
Words speak for themselves, anonymity speaks for itself.

The Unknown Master of the Pure Poem walks nightly among his
    roses,
The very garden his son laid out.
Every so often he sits down. Every so often he stands back up . . .

———————

Heavy, heavy, heavy hangs over our heads. June heat.
How many lives does it take to fabricate this one?
Aluminum pie pan bird frightener
                    dazzles and feints in a desultory breeze

Across the road, vegetable garden mojo, evil eye.
That's one life I know for sure.
Others, like insects in amber,
                    lie golden and lurking and hidden from us.

Ninety-four in the shade, humidity huge and inseparable,
Noon sun like a laser disk.
The grackle waddles forth in his suit of lights,
                            the crucifixion on his back.

———————

Affection's the absolute
                    everything rises to,
Devotion's detail, the sum of all our scatterings,
Bright imprint our lives unshadow on.

Easy enough to say that now, the hush of late spring
Hung like an after-echo

Over the neighborhood,
              devolving and disappearing.

Easy enough, perhaps, but still true,
Honeysuckle and poison ivy jumbling out of the hedge,
Magnolia beak and white tongue, landscape's off-load, love's lisp.

ENVOI

What we once liked, we no longer like.
What we used to delight in settles like fine ash on our tongues.
What we once embraced embraces us.

Things have destinies, of course,
On-lines and downloads mysterious as the language of clouds.
My life has become like that,

Half uninterpretable, half new geography,
Landscapes stilled and adumbrated, memory unratcheting,
Its voice-over not my own.

Meanwhile, the mole goes on with its subterranean daydreams,
The dogs lie around like rugs,
Birds nitpick their pinfeathers, insects slick down their shells.

No horizon-honing here, no angst in the anthill.
What happens is what happens,
And what happened to happen never existed to start with.

Still, who wants a life like that,
No next and no before, no yesterday, no today,
Tomorrow a moment no one will ever live in?

As for me, I'll take whatever wanes,
The loosening traffic on the straightaway, the dark and such,
The wandering stars, wherever they come from now, wherever
    they go.

I'll take whatever breaks down beneath its own sad weight—
The paintings of Albert Pinkham Ryder, for instance,
Language, the weather, the word of God.

I'll take as icon and testament
The daytime metaphysics of the natural world,
Sun on tie post, rock on rock.

POEM HALF IN THE MANNER OF LI HO

All things aspire to weightlessness,
                        some place beyond the lip of language,
Some silence, some zone of grace,

Sky white as raw silk,
                        opening mirror cold-sprung in the west,
Sunset like dead grass.

If God hurt the way we hurt,
                        he, too, would be heart-sore,
Disconsolate, unappeasable.

————————

Li Ho, the story goes, would leave home
Each day at dawn, riding a colt, a servant boy
                        walking behind him,
An antique tapestry bag
Strapped to his back.
                        When inspiration struck, Ho would write
The lines down and drop them in the bag.
At night he'd go home and work the lines up into a poem,
No matter how disconnected and loose-leafed they were.
His mother once said,
"He won't stop until he has vomited out his heart."

And so he did.
                Like John Keats,
He died believing his name would never be written among the
        Characters.

Without hope, he thought himself—that worst curse—unlucky.
At twenty-seven, at death's line, he saw a man come
In purple, driving a red dragon,
A tablet in one hand, who said,

                    "I'm here to summon Li Ho."
Ho got from his bed and wept.
Far from the sick room's dragon-dark, snow stormed the passes,
Monkeys surfed the bo trees

                    and foolish men ate white jade.

———————

How mournful the southern hills are,

                    how white their despair
Under December's T'ang blue blank page.

What's the use of words—there are no words
For December's chill redaction,

                    for the way it makes us feel.

We hang like clouds between heaven and earth,

                    between something and nothing,
Sometimes with shadows, sometimes without.

MEDITATION ON FORM AND MEASURE

A palm print confirms the stars, but what confirms the hand?
Out of any two thoughts I have, one is devoted to death.
Our days an uncertainty, a chaos and shapeless,
All that our lives are
                    blurs down, like a landscape reflected in water.
All stars are lights, all lights are not stars.

13 July, buck robin dry-preens on lodgepole branch,
North sky racked-over to stone-washed blue,
Star-wheels in whiteout,
One cloud over Caribou as though spray-painted there,
Doe bird tail-up under stained glass Venetian footbridge.

———

Spruce-cloister abbeyesque, trees monk-like and shadow-frocked,
Grouse in the dark folds,
Sunlight pale cross through the thick branches,
Male grouse twice-graced in a sacrificial strut,
                                        fantailed, away
From something hidden and too young, lord down the dead log.

The moon, like some albino black hole, draws the light in,
The crescent moon, falling and golden,
And darkens the sky around it erupting in stars,
Word stars, warrior stars, word warriors
                                    assembling
Accents and destinies, moon drawing the light inside.

Time and light are the same thing somewhere behind our backs.
And form is measure.
                    Without measure there is no form:
Form and measure become one.
Time and light become one somewhere beyond our future.
Father darkness, mother night,
                        one and one become one again.

Now, in their separateness, however, they sizzle and hum,
Sweet, self-destructive music
That cradles our bodies and turns them
Back to an attitude, a near-truth
Where measure is verbal architecture
                        and form is splendor.

—————

Immodestly, we pattern ourselves against the dead,
Echoes and mirrors, distant thunder,
Those fabulous constellations
                    we gaze at but can't explain.
Our lives reflections of shadows, cries
Echoes of echoes, we live among ghosts, sighting and sizing,

Hawk like a circling scrap of ash on the thermal's flame,
Gray jay non grata at feeder trough,
Barn swallows veering like fighter planes
                        out of the overcast,
La Traviata incongruous
Inside from the boom box tape, bird snarl and aria.

Memory is a cemetery
I've visited once or twice, white

                    ubiquitous and the set-aside
Everywhere under foot,
Jack robin back on his bowed branch, missus tucked butt-up
Over the eggs,

           clouds slow and deep as liners over the earth.

My life, like others' lives, has been circumscribed by stars.
O vaghe stelle dell'orso,

              beautiful stars of the Bear,
I took, one time, from a book.
Tonight, I take it again, that I, like Leopardi, might
One day immerse myself in its cold, Lethean shine.

POEM ALMOST WHOLLY IN MY OWN MANNER

Where the Southern cross the Yellow Dog
In Moorhead, Mississippi,
                         my mother sheltered her life out

In Leland, a few miles down US 82,
                             unfretted and unaware,
Layered between history and a three-line lament

About to be brought forth
                      on the wrong side of the tracks
All over the state and the Deep South.

We all know what happened next,
                      blues and jazz and rhythm-and-blues,
Then rock-and-roll, then sex-and-drugs-and-rock-and-roll, lick by lick

Blowing the lanterns out—and everything else—along the levees:
Cotton went west, the music went north
                        and everywhere in between,

Time, like a burning wheel, scorching along by the highway side,
Reorganizing, relayering,
                      turning the tenants out.

------

9 p.m. August sky eleemosynary, such sweet grief,
Music the distant thunder chord
                      that shudders our lives.

Black notes. The black notes
That follow our footsteps like blood from a cut finger.
                                                    Like that.

Fireflies, slow angel eyes,
                              nod and weave,
Tracking our chary attitudes, our malevolent mercies.

Charity, sometimes, we have,
                              appearing and disappearing
Like stars when nightwash rises through us.

(Hope and faith we lip-sync,
                              a dark dharma, a goat grace,
A grace like rain, that goes where rain goes.)

Discreetly the evening enters us,
                              overwhelms us,
As out here whatever lifts, whatever lowers, intersects.

                    ———

Interstices. We live in the cracks.
Under Ezekiel and his prophesies,
                              under the wheel.

Poetry's what's left between the lines—
                              a strange speech and a hard language,
It's all in the unwritten, it's all in the unsaid . . .

And that's a comfort, I think,
                              for our lack and inarticulation.
For our scalded flesh and our singed hair.

But what would Robert Johnson say,

                          hell-hounded and brimstone-tongued?

What would W. C. Handy say,

Those whom the wheel has overturned,

                             those whom the fire has,

And the wind has, unstuck and unstrung?

They'd say what my mother said—

                         a comfort, perhaps, but too cold

Where the Southern cross the Yellow Dog.

MEDITATION ON SUMMER AND SHAPELESSNESS

We have a bat, one bat, that bug-surfs
                              our late-summer back yard
Just as the fireflies begin
To rise, new souls, toward the August moon.
Flap-limbed, ungathered,
He stumbles unerringly through them,
Exempt as they feint and ascend to their remission—
Light, Catharist light;
Brightness to brightness where I sit
                              on the back brink of my sixth decade,
Virginia moon in the cloud-ragged, cloud-scutted sky,
Bat bug-drawn and swallow-crossed, God's wash.

One comes to understand
                              Candide and Tiberius,
Sour saints, aspiring aphasiacs,
Recluses and anchorites,
Those whom the moon's pull and the moon's
                                        hydrointerpretation
Crumble twice under,
Those hard few for whom the Eagle has never landed.
Out here, all's mythic, medieval, or early A.D.
One half expects
                    Raymond of Toulouse or Hadrian to step forth,
Resplendent and otherwise, out of the hedge row or arborvitae.
One half hopes, moon's gun with a dead bead.

————

I never quite got it, what they meant,
                              but now I do,

Waking each morning at dawn,
Or before, some shapeless, unfingerprintable dread
On me like cold-crossed humidity,
Extinction shouldering, like a season, in from my dreamscape.
Without my glasses, the light around the window shade
Throbs like an aura, so faint
At first, then luminous with its broken promises—
Feckless icon, dark reliquary.
Mortality hunches, like fine furniture, crowding the room.

Rising, feeding the dogs, bringing the newspaper in,
Somehow should loosen things up.
It doesn't, of course.
                              There's still the pill to be taken,
And then another, eye drops,
Toothbrush and toothpaste,
                              reflection of someone older and strange
Constantly in the mirror,
Breakfast and then the day's doom, long-leafed
And everywhere,
Shadowing what I look at, shadowing what I see.
The News, then supper, then back to the black beginning.

                    ————

Après-dog days, dead end of August,
Summer a holding pattern,
                              heat, haze, humidity
The mantra we still chant, the bell-tick our tongues all toll.
Whatever rises becomes a light—
Firefly and new moon,
Star and star and star chart
                              unscrolled across the heavens
Like radioactive dump sites bulb-lit on a map.

Whatever holds back goes dark—
The landscape and all its accoutrements, my instinct, my hands,
My late, untouchable hands.

Summer's crepuscular, rot and wrack,
Rain-ravaged, root-ruined.
Each August the nightscape inserts itself
                                    another inch in my heart,
Piece and a piece, piecemeal, time's piecework.
August unedges and polishes me, water's way.
Such subtle lapidary.
Last lights go out in the next-door house,
                            dogs disappear,
Privet and white pine go under, bird-squelch and frog-shrill.
To be separate, to be apart, is to be whole again.
Full night now and dust sheet—
                        the happy life is the darkened life.

THE APPALACHIAN BOOK OF THE DEAD

Sunday, September Sunday . . . Outdoors,
Like an early page from The Appalachian Book of the Dead,
Sunlight lavishes brilliance on every surface,
Doves settle, surreptitious angels, on tree limb and box branch,
A crow calls, deep in its own darkness,
Something like water ticks on
Just there, beyond the horizon, just there, steady clock . . .

Go in fear of abstractions . . .
                              Well, possibly. Meanwhile,
They *are* the strata our bodies rise through, the sere veins
Our skins rub off on.
For instance, whatever enlightenment there might be
Housels compassion and affection, those two tributaries
That river above our lives,
Whose waters we sense the sense of
                              late at night, and later still.

Uneasy, suburbanized,
I drift from the lawn chair to the back porch to the dwarf orchard
Testing the grass and border garden.
A stillness, as in the passageways of Paradise,
Bell jars the afternoon.
                    Leaves, like *ex votos,* hang hard and shine
Under the endlessness of heaven.
Such skeletal altars, such vacant sanctuary.

It always amazes me
How landscape recalibrates the stations of the dead,

How what we see jacks up

the odd quotient of what we don't see,

How God's breath reconstitutes our walking up and walking down.

First glimpse of autumn, stretched tight and snicked, a bad face lift,

Flicks in and flicks out,

a virtual reality.

Time to begin the long division.

UMBRIAN DREAMS

Nothing is flat-lit and tabula rasaed in Charlottesville,
Umbrian sackcloth,
           stigmata and *Stabat mater,*
A sleep and a death away,
Night, and a sleep and a death away—
Light's frost-fired and Byzantine here,
                    aureate, beehived,
Falling in Heraclitean streams
Through my neighbor's maple trees.
There's nothing medieval and two-dimensional in our town,
October in full drag, Mycenaean masked and golden lobed.

Like Yeats, however, I dream of a mythic body,
Feathered and white, a landscape
                horizoned and honed as an anchorite.
(Iacopo, hear me out, St. Francis, have you a word for me?)
Umbrian lightfall, lambent and ichorous, mists through my days,
As though a wound, somewhere and luminous,
                  flickered and went out,
Flickered and went back out—
So weightless the light, so stretched and pained,
It seems to ooze, and then not ooze, down from that one hurt.
You doubt it? Look. Put your finger there. No, there. You see?

OCTOBER II

October in mission creep,
                              autumnal reprise and stand down.
The more reality takes shape, the more it loses intensity—
Synaptic uncertainty,
Electrical surge and quick lick of the minus sign,
Tightening of the force field
Wherein our forms are shaped and shapes formed,
                              wherein we pare ourselves to our attitudes . . .

Do not despair—one of the thieves was saved; do not presume—
        one of the thieves was damned,
Wrote Beckett, quoting St. Augustine.
It was the shape of the sentence he liked, the double iambic
        pentameter:
It is the shape that matters, he said.
Indeed, shape precludes shapelessness, as God precludes
        Godlessness.
Form is the absence of all things. Like sin. Yes, like sin.

It's the shape beneath the shape that summons us, the juice
That spreads the rose, the multifoliate spark
                              that drops the leaf
And darkens our entranceways,
The rush that transfigures the maple tree,
                              the rush that transubstantiates our lives.
October, the season's signature and garnishee,
October, the exponential negative, the plus.

LIVES OF THE SAINTS

1

A loose knot in a short rope,
My life keeps sliding out from under me, intact but
Diminishing,
               its pattern becoming patternless,
The blue abyss of everyday air
Breathing it in and breathing it out,
                       in little clouds like smoke,
In little wind strings and threads.

Everything that the pencil says is erasable,
Unlike our voices, whose words are black and permanent,
Smudging our lives like coal dust,
                   unlike our memories,
Etched like a skyline against the mind,
Unlike our irretrievable deeds . . .
The pencil spills everything, and then takes everything back.

For instance, here I am at Hollywood Boulevard and Vine,
Almost 60, Christmas Eve, the flesh-flashers and pimps
And inexhaustible Walk of Famers
                   snubbing their joints out,
Hoping for something not-too-horrible to happen across the street.
The rain squall has sucked up and bumped off,
The palm fronds dangle lubriciously.
                     Life, as they say, is beautiful.

One week into 1995, and all I've thought about
Is endings, retreads,
                              the love of loss
Light as a locket around my neck, idea of absence
Hard and bright as a dime inside my trouser pocket.
Where is the new and negotiable,
The undiscovered snapshot,
                              the phoneme's refusal, word's rest?

Remember, face the facts, Miss Stein said.
                              And so I've tried,
Pretending there's nothing there but description, hoping emotion
     shows;
That that's why description's there:
The subject was never smoke,
                              there's always been a fire.
The winter dark shatters around us like broken glass.
The morning sky opens its pink robe.

All explorers must die of heartbreak.
                              Middle-aged poets, too,
Wind from the northwest, small wind,
Two crows in the ash tree, one on an oak limb across the street.
Endless effortless nothingness, January blue:
Noteless measureless music;
                              imageless iconography.
I'll be the lookout and listener, you do the talking . . .

3

Chinook, the January thaw;

                    warm wind from the Gulf
Spinning the turn-around and dead leaves
Northeast and southeast—
I like it under the trees in winter,

                           everything over me dead,
Or half-dead, sky hard,
Wind moving the leaves around clockwise, then counterclockwise too.

We live in a place that is not our own . . .

                       I'll say . . . Roses rot
In the side garden's meltdown, shrubs bud,
The sounds of syllables altogether elsewhere rise
Like white paint through the sun—

                    familiar only with God,
We yearn to be pierced by that
Occasional void through which the supernatural flows.

The plain geometry of the dead does not equate,
Infinite numbers, untidy sums:
We believe in belief but don't believe,

                   for which we shall be judged.
In winter, under the winter trees—
A murder of crows glides over, some thirty or more,
To its appointment,

            sine and cosine, angle and arc.

The winter wind re-nails me,
                    respirations of the divine
In and out, a cold fusion.
Such dire lungs.
The sun goes up and the sun goes down,
                    small yelps from the short weeds.
Listen up, Lord, listen up.
The night birds sleep with their wings ajar.
                    Black branches, black branches.

Al poco giorno ed al gran cerchio d'ombra—
A little light and a great darkness,
Darkness wherein our friends are hid,
                    and our love's gone wrong.
If death is abstract (force through pure, illusory space),
May I be put, when the time comes, in the dwelling of St. John
As I wrest myself from joy
                    into the meta-optics of desire.

Posteriori Dei . . .
God's back, love's loss, light's blank the eye can accommodate
And the heart shelve,
                    world's ever-more-disappearing vacancy
Under the slow-drag clouds of heaven
The landscape absorbs and then repents of,
                    clouds ponderous as a negative
Nothing can keep from moving.

The afternoon is urban, and somewhat imaginary,
Behind the snowfall, winter's printout
And self-defense, its matrix and self-design.

All afternoon

The afternoon was ordinary
And self-perpetuating behind its Chinese screen.
But it was urban, and actual, in the long run.

In dread we stay and in dread depart . . .

Not much wrench room.

The 13th century knew this, a movable floor—
Here's bad and There's worse.
Outside the door, demons writhed just under the earth's crust,
Outside the door,

and licensed to govern in God's name.

On the street, the ride-bys and executions lip-chant and sing.

Contemplative, cloistered, tongue-tied,

Zen says, watch your front.

Zen says, wherever you are is a monastery.
The afternoon says, life's a loose knot in a short rope.
The afternoon says,

show me your hands, show me your feet.

The lives of the saints become our lives.
God says, watch your back.

CHRISTMAS EAST OF THE BLUE RIDGE

So autumn comes to an end with these few wet sad stains
Stuck to the landscape,
$\qquad$ December dark
Running its hands through the lank hair of late afternoon,
Little tongues of the rain holding forth
$\qquad$ under the eaves,
Such wash, such watery words . . .

So autumn comes to this end,
And winter's vocabulary, downsized and distanced,
Drop by drop
Captures the conversation with its monosyllabic gutturals
And tin music,
$\qquad$ gravelly consonants, scratched vowels.

Soon the camel drivers will light their fires, soon the stars
Will start on their brief dip down from the back of heaven,
Down to the desert's dispensation
And night reaches, the gall and first birth,
The second only one word from now,
$\qquad$ one word and its death from right now.

Meanwhile, in Charlottesville, the half-moon
Hums like a Hottentot
$\qquad$ high over Monticello,
Clouds dishevel and rag out,
The alphabet of our discontent
Keeps on with its lettering,
$\qquad$ gold on the black walls of our hearts . . .

NEGATIVES II

One erases only in order to write again . . .

You don't know what you don't know,
We used to say in the CIC in Verona—
Negative space, negative operability
To counterposition the white drift of the unknown.
You can't see what you can't see.

It's still the best advice, but easy to overlook
As winter grinds out its cigarette
Across the landscape.
                              February.
Who could have known, in 1959, the balloon would not go up?
Who could have seen, back then, the new world's new disorder?

John Ruskin says all clouds are masses of light, even the darkest ones.
Hard to remember that these overcast afternoons,
Midweek, ash-black and ash-white,
                                            negative shapes sketched in
And luminous here and there in loose interstices
Elbowed and stacked between earth and sky.

Hard to remember that as the slipstream of memory shifts
And shutters, massing what wasn't there as though it were.
Where are the secret codes these days for nuking the Brenner Pass?
And the Run, and the Trieste Station?
Like sculptured mist, sharp-edged and cut into form, they slide on by.

One only writes in order to erase again . . .

LIVES OF THE ARTISTS

1

Learn how to model before you learn to finish things,
Michelangelo hisses . . .

                    Before you bear witness,
Be sure you have something that calls for a witnessing,
I might add—
Don't gloss what isn't assignable or brought to bear,
Don't shine what's expendable.

March in the northern south. Hard ides-heat
Bangs through the branches of winter trees,

                             thumps the gauges
Needling green and immodestly
Out of the dead leaves, out of their opium half-dreams.
Willows, medusa-hooded and bone-browed, begin to swim up
Through their brown depths, wasps revive

                    and plants practice their scales.

In Poussin's apocalypse,

                    we're all merely emanations sent forth
From landscape's hell-hung heart-screen—
Some flee through the dust, some find them a bed in the wind's
    scorched mouth,
Some disappear in flame . . .

                  As I do this afternoon
Under the little fires in the plum tree, white-into-white-into-white,
Unidentified bird on a limb, lung-light not of this world.

2

When you have died there will be nothing—
No memory of you will remain,

                  not even a trace as you walk
Aimlessly, unseen, in the fitful halls of the dead,
Sappho warns us. She also writes:
The moon has set, and the Pleiades—

                  in the deep middle of the night
The time is passing . . .

How is it that no one remembers this?

                  Time's ashes, *I lie alone.*
So simple, so simple, so unlike the plastic ticking Christ
Who preyed on us we prayed to—
Such eucharistic side-bars, such saint-shortened anomalies
Under the dull stained glass,

                down the two-lane and four-lane highways.
Pain enters me drop by drop.

The two plum trees, like tired angels, have *dropped their wings at*
    their sides.
I walk quietly among the autumn offerings
Dark hands from the underworld
Push up around me,

            gold-amber cups
and bittersweet, nightshade, indulgences from the dead.
I walk quietly and carefully on their altar,

                among their prayers.

3

We all rise, if we rise at all, to what we're drawn by,
Big Smoke, simplicity's signature,
Last untranslatable text—
The faithful do not speak many words . . .
                                        What's there to say,
Little smoke, cloud-smoke, in the plum trees,
Something's name indecipherable
                        rechalked in the scrawled branches.

Everything God possesses, it's been said, *the wise man already has.*
Some slack, then, some hope.
Don't give the word to everyone,
The gift is tiny, the world made up
Of deceivers and those who are deceived—
                                        the true word
Is the word about the word.

Celestial gossip, celestial similes
(Like, like, like, like, like)
Powder the plum blossoms nervously, invisibly,
                                        the word
In hiding, unstirred. The facts,
The bits of narrative,
                        glow, intermittent and flaked.
The sins of the uninformed are the first shame of their teachers.

4

Jaundicing down from their purity, the plum blossoms
Snowfall out of the two trees
And spread like a sheet of mayflies
                              soundlessly, thick underfoot—
I am the silence that is incomprehensible,
First snow stars drifting down from the sky,
                              late fall in the other world;
I am the utterance of my name.

Belief in transcendence,
                    belief in something beyond belief,
Is what the blossoms solidify
In their fall through the two worlds—
The imaging of the invisible, the slow dream of metaphor,
Sanction our going up and our going down, our days
And the lives we infold inside them,
                              our *yes* and *yes.*

Good to get that said, tongue of cold air
Licking the landscape,
                    snuffing the flame in the green fuse.
I am the speech that cannot be grasped.
I am the substance and the thing that has no substance,
Cast forth upon the face of the earth,
Whose margins we write in,
                    whose one story we tell, and keep on telling.

There's nothing out there but light,
                              the would-be artist said,
As usual just half right:
There's also a touch of darkness, everyone knows, on both sides
    of both horizons,
Prescribed and unpaintable,
Touching our fingertips whichever way we decide to jump.
His small palette, however, won't hold that color,
                    though some have, and some still do.

The two plum trees know nothing of that,
Having come to their green grief,
                          their terrestrial touch-and-go,
Out of grace and radiance,
Their altered bodies alteration transmogrified.
Mine is a brief voice, a still, brief voice
Unsubject to change or the will to change—
                        might it be restrung and rearranged.

But that is another story.
                    Vasari tells us
An earlier tale than Greek of the invention of painting,
How Gyges of Lydia
Once saw his own shadow cast
                    by the light of a fire
And instantly drew his own outline on the wall with charcoal . . .
Learn to model before you learn how to finish things.

DEEP MEASURE

Shank of the afternoon, wan weight-light,
Undercard of a short month,
                              February Sunday . . .
Wordlessness of the wrong world.
In the day's dark niche, the patron saint of What-Goes-Down
Shuffles her golden deck and deals,
                              one for you and one for me . . .

And that's it, a single number—we play what we get.
My hand says measure,
                              doves on the wire and first bulb blades
Edging up through the mulch mat,
Inside-out of the winter gum trees,
A cold harbor, cold stop and two-step, and here it comes,

Deep measure,
                 deep measure that runnels beneath the bone,
That sways our attitude and sets our lives to music;
Deep measure, down under and death-drawn:
Pilgrim, homeboy of false time,
Listen and set your foot down,
                              listen and step lightly.

THINKING OF WINTER
AT THE BEGINNING OF SUMMER

Milton paints purple trees. Avery.

                      And Wolf Kahn too.

I've liked their landscapes,
Nightdreams and daymares,

                      pastures and woods that burn our eyes.

Otherwise, why would we look?
Otherwise, why would we stretch our hands out and gather them in?

My brother slides through the blue zones in enormous planes.
My sister's cartilage, ash and bone.
My parents rock in their blackened boats

                      back and forth, back and forth.

Above the ornamental cherries, the sky is a box and a glaze.
Well, yes, a box and a glaze.

Pulled from despair like a bad tooth,
I see my roots, tiny roots,

                      glisten like good luck in the sun.

What we refuse defines us,

                  a little of this, a little of that.

The light stays fool's gold for a long time.
The light stays fool's gold for a long time.

                             —For Winter Wright

JESUIT GRAVES

Midsummer. Irish overcast. Oatmeal-colored sky.
The Jesuit pit. Last mass
For hundreds whose names are incised on the marble wall
Above the gravel and grassless dirt.
Just dirt and the small stones—
                              how strict, how self-effacing.

Not suited for you, however, Father Bird-of-Paradise,
Whose *plumage of far wonder* is not formless and not faceless,
Whatever you might have hoped for once.
Glasnevin Cemetery, Dublin, 3 July 1995.
For those who would rise to meet their work,
                              that work is scaffolding.

Sacrifice is the cause of ruin.
The absence of sacrifice is the cause of ruin.
Thus the legends instruct us,
North wind through the flat-leaved limbs of the sheltering trees,
Three desperate mounds in the small, square enclosure,
                        souls God-gulped and heaven-hidden.

P. Gerardus Hopkins, 28 July 1844–8 June 1889, Age 44.
And then the next name. And then the next,
Soldiers of misfortune, lock-step into a star-colored tight dissolve,
History's hand-me-ons. But you, Father Candescence,
You, Father Fire?
                    Whatever rises comes together, they say. They say.

MEDITATION ON SONG AND STRUCTURE

I love to wake to the *coo coo* of the mourning dove
At dawn—
                    like one drug masking another's ill effects,
It tells me that everything's all right when I know that everything's
     wrong.
It lays out the landscape's hash marks,
                                        the structures of everyday.
It makes what's darkened unworkable
For that moment, and that, as someone once said, is grace.
But this bird's a different story.

Dawn in the Umbrian hills.
In the cracks of the persian blinds, slim ingots of daylight stack
     and drip.
This bird has something to say—
                              a watery kind of music,
Extended improvisations, liquid riffs and breaks—
But not to me, pulled like a dead weight
From the riptide of sleep, not to me,
Depression's darling, history's hand job, not to me . . .

                    ————

Twice, now, I've heard the nightingale.
                              First in the first light
Of a dust-grey dawn,
And then at midnight, a week later,
Walking my friend to the parking lot
In Todi, moon vamping behind the silted cloud mounds,
A pentimento of sudden illumination,

Like bird work or spider work.

      Senti, my friend said, *Shhh,*

È l'usignolo, the nightingale,
As bird and bird song drifted downhill,

        easy as watershine,
Ripply and rock-run.
Silence. No moon, no motorbike, no bird.
The silence of something come and something gone away.
Nightingale, ghost bird, ghost song,
Hand that needles and threads the night together,

        light a candle for me.

————

Swallows over the battlements

      and thigh-moulded red tile roofs,
Square crenelations, Guelph town.
Swallows against the enfrescoed backdrop of tilled hills
Like tiny sharks in the tinted air
That buoys them like a tide,

      arrested, water-colored surge.
Swallows darting like fish through the alabaster air,
Cleansing the cleanliness, feeding on seen and the unseen.

To come back as one of them!
Loose in the light and landscape-shine,

       language without words,
Ineffable part of the painting and ignorant of it,
Pulled by the lunar landswell,
Demi-denizen of the godhead
Spread like a golden tablecloth wherever you turn—
Such judgment, such sweet witch-work.

————

This mockingbird's got his chops.
Bird song over black water—
Am I south or north of my own death,

west or east of my final hurt?
In North Carolina, half a century ago,
Bird song over black water,
Lake Llewellyn Bibled and night-colored,

mockingbird
Soul-throated, like light, a little light in great darkness.

Zodiac damped, then clicked off,

cloud-covering-heaven.
Bird song over black water.
I remember the way the song contained many songs,
As it does now, the same song
Over the tide pool of my neighbor's yard, and mine's slack turning,
Many songs, a season's worth,
Many voices, a light to lead back

to silence, sound of the first voice.

———

Medieval, prelatic, why
Does the male cardinal sing that song, *omit, omit,*
From the eminence of the gum tree?
What is it he knows,

silence, *omit, omit,* silence,
The afternoon breaking away in little pieces,
Siren's squeal from the bypass,
The void's tattoo, *Nothing Matters,*

mottoed across our white hearts?

Nature abhors originality, according to Cioran.
Landscape desires it, I say,

The back yard unloading its cargo of solitudes
Into the backwash of last light—
Cardinal, exhale my sins,

                     help me to lie low and leave out,
Remind me that vision is singular, that excess
Is regress, that more than enough is too much, that

                                   compression is all.

SITTING AT DUSK IN THE BACK YARD
AFTER THE MONDRIAN RETROSPECTIVE

Form imposes, structure allows—
                        the slow destruction of form
So as to bring it back resheveled, reorganized,
Is the hard heart of the enterprise.
                             Under its camouflage,
The light, relentless shill and cross-dresser, pools and deals.
Inside its short skin, the darkness burns.

Mondrian thought the destructive element in art
Much too neglected.
                       Landscape, of course, pursues it savagely.
And that's what he meant:
You can't reconstruct without the destruction being built in;
There is no essence unless
                     nothing has been left out.

Destruction takes place so order might exist.
                             Simple enough.
Destruction takes place at the point of maximum awareness.
Orate sine intermissione, St. Paul instructs.
Pray uninterruptedly.
The gods and their names have disappeared.
                           Only the clouds remain.

Meanwhile, the swallows wheel, the bat wheels, the grackles
    begin their business.
It's August.
        The countryside

Gathers itself for sacrifice, its slow

                                     fadeout along the invisible,

Leaving the land its architecture of withdrawal,

Black lines and white spaces, an emptiness primed with reds and blues.

BLACK ZODIAC

Darkened by time, the masters, like our memories, mix
And mismatch,
           and settle about our lawn furniture, like air
Without a meaning, like air in its clear nothingness.
What can we say to either of them?
How can they be so dark and so clear at the same time?
They ruffle our hair,
           they ruffle the leaves of the August trees.
Then stop, abruptly as wind.
The flies come back, and the heat—
           what can we say to them?
Nothing is endless but the sky.
The flies come back, and the afternoon
Teeters a bit on its green edges,
           then settles like dead weight
Next to our memories, and the pale hems of the masters' gowns.

———

Those who look for the Lord will cry out in praise of him.
Perhaps. And perhaps not—
           dust and ashes though we are,
Some will go worldlessly, some
Will listen their way in with their mouths
Where pain puts them, an inch-and-a-half above the floor.
And some will revile him out of love
           and deep disdain.
The gates of mercy, like an eclipse, darken our undersides.
Rows of gravestones stay our steps,
           August humidity

Bright as auras around our bodies.
And some will utter the words,

                              speaking in fear and tongues,
Hating their garments splotched by the flesh.
These are the lucky ones, the shelved ones, the twice-erased.

———————

Dante and John Chrysostom
Might find this afternoon a sidereal roadmap,
A pilgrim's way . . .
                    You might too
Under the prejaundiced outline of the quarter moon,
Clouds sculling downsky like a narrative for *whatever comes,*
What *hasn't happened to happen yet*
Still lurking behind the stars,
                              31 August 1995 . . .
The afterlife of insects, space graffiti, white holes
In the landscape,
                    such things, such avenues, lead to dust
And handle our hurt with ease.
Sky blue, blue of infinity, blue
                              waters above the earth:
Why do the great stories always exist in the past?

———————

The unexamined life's no different from
                              the examined life—
Unanswerable questions, small talk,
Unprovable theorems, long-abandoned arguments—
You've got to write it all down.
Landscape or waterscape, light-length on evergreen, dark sidebar
Of evening,
            you've got to write it down.

Memory's handkerchief, death's dream and automobile,
God's sleep,
                 you've still got to write it down,
Moon half-empty, moon half-full,
Night starless and egoless, night blood-black and prayer-black,
Spider at work between the hedges,
Last bird call,
                 toad in a damp place, tree frog in a dry . . .

————

We go to our graves with secondary affections,
Second-hand satisfaction, half-souled,
                              star charts demagnetized.
We go in our best suits. The birds are flying. Clouds pass.
Sure we're cold and untouchable,
                              but we harbor no ill will.
No tooth tuned to resentment's fork,
                         we're out of here, and sweet meat.
Calligraphers of the disembodied, God's word-wards,
What letters will we illuminate?
Above us, the atmosphere,
The nothing that's nowhere, signs on, and waits for our beck and
    call.
Above us, the great constellations sidle and wince,
The letters undarken and come forth,
Your X and my X.
                    The letters undarken and they come forth.

————

Eluders of memory, nocturnal sleep of the greenhouse,
Spirit of slides and silences,
                         Invisible Hand,
Witness and walk on.

Lords of the discontinuous, lords of the little gestures,
Succor my shift and save me . . .
All afternoon the rain has rained down in the mind,
And in the gardens and dwarf orchard.

                                      All afternoon
The lexicon of late summer has turned its pages
Under the rain,

                    abstracting the necessary word.
Autumn's upon us.
The rain fills our narrow beds.
Description's an element, like air or water.

                              That's the word.

CHINA MAIL

It's deep summer east of the Blue Ridge.
Temperatures over 90 for the twenty-fifth day in a row.
The sound of the asphalt trucks down Locust Avenue
Echoes between the limp trees.
                              Nothing's cool to the touch.

Since you have not come,
The way back will stay unknown to you.
And since you have not come,
                              I find I've become like you,
A cloud whose rain has all fallen, adrift and floating.

Walks in the great void are damp and sad.
Late middle age. With little or no work,
                              we return to formlessness,
The beginning of all things.
Study the absolute, your book says. But not too hard,

I add, just under my breath.
Cicadas ratchet their springs up to a full stop
                              in the green wings of the oaks.
This season is called white hair.
Like murdered moonlight, it keeps coming back from the dead.

Our lives will continue to turn unmet,
                              like Virgo and Scorpio.
Of immortality, there's nothing but old age and its aftermath.
It's better you never come.
How else would we keep in touch, tracing our words upon the air?

DISJECTA MEMBRA

1

Back yard, dry flower half-border, unpeopled landscape
Stripped of embellishment and anecdotal concern:
A mirror of personality,
                          unworldly and self-effacing,
The onlooker sees himself in,
                              a monk among the oak trees . . .
How silly, the way we place ourselves—the struck postures,
The soothing words, the sleights-of-hand
                                  to hoodwink the Paraclete—
For our regard; how always the objects we draw out
To show ourselves to effect
(The chiaroscuro of character we yearn for)
Find us a shade untrue and a shade untied.
                          Bad looking glass, bad things.

———————

Simplify, Shaker down, the voice drones.
Out of the aether, disembodied and discontent,
No doubt who *that* is . . .
                          Autumn prehensile from day one,
Equinox pushing through like a cold front from the west,
Drizzle and dropped clouds, wired wind.
It's Sunday again, brief devotions.
We look down, dead leaves and dead grass like a starry sky
From inside out.
                    Simplify, open the emptiness, divest—
The trees do, each year milking their veins

Down, letting the darkness drip in,
                              I.V. from the infinite.

—————

Filing my nails in the Buddha yard.
Ten feet behind my back, like slow, unsteady water,
Backwash of traffic spikes and falls off,
Zendo half-hunched through the giant privet,
                              shut sure as a shell.
Last cat's-eyes of dew crystal and gold as morning fills the grass.
Between Buddha-stare and potting shed,
Indian file of ants. Robin's abrupt arrival
And dust-down.
                    Everything's one with everything else now,
Wind leaf-lifter and tuck-in,
Light giving over to shadow and shadow to light.

—————

I hope for a second chance where the white clouds are born,
Where the maple trees turn red,
                              redder by half than where
The flowers turned red in spring.
Acolyte at the altar of wind,
I love the idleness of the pine tree,
                              the bright steps into the sky.
I've always wanted to lie there, as though under earth,
Blood drops like sapphires, the dark stations ahead of me
Like postal stops on a deep journey.
I long for that solitude,
                    that rest,
The bed-down and rearrangement of all the heart's threads.

—————

What nurtures us denatures us and will strip us down.
Zen says, stand by the side of your thoughts
As you might stand by the bank of a wide river.
                                              Dew-burdened,
Spider webs spin like little galaxies in the juniper bush,
Morning sunlight corpus delicti
                                   sprawled on the damp pavement.
Denatures us to a nub.
And sends us twisting out of our back yards into history.
As though by a wide river,
                              water hustling our wants away,
And what we're given, and what we hope to be absolved of . . .
How simply it moves, how silently.

                              ————

Death's still the secret of life,
                                   the garden reminds us.
Or vice-versa. It's complicated.
Unlike the weed-surge and blossom-surge of early fall,
Unlike the insect husks in the spider's tracery,
Crickets and rogue crows gearing up for afternoon sing-along.
The cottontail hides
                        out in the open, hunched under the apple tree
Between the guillotine of sunlight and guillotine of shade
Beyond my neighbor's hedge.
                              The blades rise and the blades fall,
But rabbit sits tight. Smart bun.
Sit tight and hold on. Sit tight. Hold on.

                              ————

Love is more talked about than surrendered to. Lie low,
Meng Chiao advises—
                        beauty too close will ruin your life.

Like the south wind, it's better to roam without design.
A lifetime's a solitary thread, we all learn,

                              and needs its knot tied.
Under the arborvitae,
The squirrels have buried their winter dreams,

                      and ghosts gather, close to home.
My shadow sticks to the trees' shadow.
There is no simile for this,

                      this black into black.
Or if there is, it's my penpoint's drop of ink slurred to a word.
Of both, there soon will be not a trace.

———————

With what words, with what silence—
Silence becoming speechlessness,

                      words being nothing at all—
Can we address a blade of grass, the immensity of a snowflake?
How is it that we presume so much?

                      There are times, Lord, there are times . . .
We must bite hard into the 21st century,
We must make it bleed.
October approaches the maple trees with its laying-on of hands,
Red stains in the appled west,

                      red blush beginning to seep through
Just north of north, arterial headway, cloud on cloud.
Let it come, Lord, let it come.

2

If I could slide into a deep sleep,
I could say—to myself, without speaking—why my words
    embarrass me.

Nothing regenerates us, or shapes us again from the dust.
Nothing whispers our name in the night.
Still must we praise you, nothing,
                    still must we call to you.

Our sin is lack of transparency.

November is dark and doom-dangled,
                    fitful bone light
And suppuration, worn wrack
In the trees, dog rot and dead leaves, watch where you're going . . .

Illegibility. Dumb fingers from a far hand.

————

When death completes the number of the body, its food
Is weeping and much groaning,
                    and stranglers come, who roll
Souls down on the dirt . . .
                And thus it is written, and thus believed,
Though others have found it otherwise.

The restoration of the nature of the ones who are good
Takes place in a time that never had a beginning.

Well, yes, no doubt about that.
One comes to rest in whatever is at rest, and eats

The food he has hungered for.
The light that shines forth there, on that body, does not sink.

————

This earth is a handful of sleep, eyes open, eyes shut,
A handful, just that—

There is an end to things, but not here.
It's where our names are, hanging like flesh from the flame trees.

Still, there are no flame points in the sky—

There are no angels, there is no light
At just that point where one said,

                    this is where light begins.

It dies out in me.

The word is inscribed in the heart.

                    It is beyond us,
The heart, that changeling, word within word.

————

Compulsive cameo, God's blue breath
So light on the skin, so infinite,

Why do I have to carry you, unutterable?
Why do you shine out,

                    lost penny, unspendable thing,

Irreversible, unappeasable, luminous,
Recoursed on the far side of language?

Tomorrow's our only hiding place,
November its last address—

                  such small griefs, such capture.

Insurmountable comforts.
And still I carry you. And still you continue to shine out.

—————

Substance. And absence of all substance.
God's not concerned for anything, and has no desire.

Late at night we feel,
                  insensate, immaculata,
The cold, coercive touch of nothing, whose fingerprints
Adhere like watermarks to the skin—

Late at night, our dark and one refuge.

Life is a sore gain, no word, no world.
Eternity drips away, inch by inch, inside us,
December blitzing our blind side,
                       white-tongued and anxious.

That's it. Something licks us up.

—————

December. Blood rolls back to its wound.
God is a scattered part,
               syllable after syllable, his name asunder.

No first heaven, no second.
Winter sun is a killer,
              late light bladed horizon-like

Wherever you turn,
                              arteried, membraned, such soft skin.

Prayers afflict us, this world and the next:

Grief's an eclipse, it comes and it goes.
Photographs show that stars are born as easily as we are.
Both without mercy.

Each leads us away, leads us away.

                              _____

Guilt is a form in itself.
                              As is the love of sentences
That guilt resides in, then darkens.
                                        It is as certain.
It is as unregenerative. It is as worn.

Everything terminal has hooks in eternity.
Marsh grass, for instance. Foxfire.
Root work and come-betweens,
                              the Lord's welkin and Lord's will,

As some say in these parts not out loud.

In the bare tines of the lemon tree,
Thorns bristle and nubs nudge,
                              limbs in a reverie of lost loads.
This life is our set-aside, our dry spot and shelter.

                              _____

When slant-light crisps up,
                              and shatters like broken lime glass

Through the maple trees, in December,
Who cares about anything but weights and absolutes?

Write up, it's bad, write down, it's still bad.
Remember, everyone's no one.

The abyss of time is a white glove—
                                    take it off, put it on,
Finger by finger it always fits,
Buttons mother-of-pearl, so snug, such soft surroundings.

Lord of the broken oak branch,
                                    Lord of the avenues,
Tweak and restartle me, guide my hand.

3

Whatever it was I had to say,
                    I've said two times, and then a third.
An object for light to land on,
                    I'm one-on-one with the visible
And shadowy overhang.
It's Christmas Eve, and the Pleiades
Burn like high altar host flames
                    scrunched in the new moon sky—
Their earthly, votive counterparts flash and burst in the spruce trees
And Mrs. Fornier's window.
It's 9:10 and I'm walking the dogs down Locust Avenue.
It's a world we've memorized by heart:
Myopic constellations, dog's bark,
                    bleak supplicants, blood of the lamb . . .

———

Unfinished, unable, distracted—
How easily we reproach ourselves for our lives lived badly,
How easily us undo.
Despair is our consolation, sweet word,
                    and late middle age
And objectivity dulled and drear.
Splendor of little fragments.
Rilke knew one or two things about shame and unhappiness
And how we waste time and worse.
I think I'm starting to catch on myself.
                    I think I'm starting to understand
The difference between the adjective and the noun.

———

Dead moth, old metaphysician, cross-backed, Christ's arrowhead,
    look,
I'll tell you one thing—
Inch by inch, everyday, our lives become less and less.
Obsessive and skinless, we shrink them down.
And here's another—
                    a line of poetry's a line of blood.
A cross on the back is like a short sword in the heart,
December sun in a fadeaway, cloud under cloud
Over the Blue Ridge,
                just there, just west of Bremo Bluff.
Okay, I'll keep my mouth shut and my eyes fast on the bare
    limbs of the fruit trees.
A line in the earth's a life.

——————

O well the snow falls and small birds drop out of the sky,
The back yard's a winding sheet—
                    winter in Charlottesville,
Epiphany two days gone,
Nothing at large but Broncos, pickups and 4x4s.
Even the almost full moon
              is under a monochrome counterpane
Of dry grey.
           Eve of St. Agnes and then some, I'd say,
Twenty-three inches and coming down.
The Rev. Doctor Syntax puts finger to forehead on the opposite
    wall,
Mancini and I still blurred beside him, Mykonos, 1961,
The past a snowstorm the present too.

——————

The human position—anxiety's afterlife, still place—
Escapes us.
          We live in the wind-chill,
The what-if and what-was-not,
The blown and sour dust of just after or just before,
The metaquotidian landscape
                    of soft edge and abyss.
How hard to take the hard day and ease it in our hearts,
Its icicle and snowdrift and
                  its wind that keeps on blowing.
How hard to be as human as snow is, or as true,
So sure of its place and many names.
It holds the white light against its body, it benights our eyes.

———

The poem uncurls me, corrects me and croons my tune,
Its outfit sharp as the pressed horizon.
                    Excessive and honed,
It grins like a blade,
It hums like a fuse,
          body of ash, body of fire,
A music my ear would be heir to.
I glimpse it now and then through the black branches of winter trees.
I hear its burn in the still places.
Halfway through January, sky pure, sky not so pure,
World still in tucker and bib.
Might I slipstream its fiery ride,
               might I mind its smoke.

———

Is *this* the life we long for,
             to be at ease in the natural world,

Blue rise of Blue Ridge
Indented and absolute through the January oak limbs,
Turkey buzzard at work on road-kill opossum, up
And flapping each time
A car passes and coming back
                              huge and unfolded, a black bed sheet,
Crows fierce but out of focus high up in the ash tree,
Afternoon light from stage left
Low and listless, little birds
Darting soundlessly back and forth, hush, hush?
                              Well, yes, I think so.

Take a loose rein and a deep seat,
                              John, my father-in-law, would say
To someone starting out on a long journey, meaning, take it easy,
Relax, let what's taking you take you.
I think of landscape incessantly,
                              mountains and rivers, lost lakes
Where sunsets festoon and override,
The scald of summer wheat fields, light-licked and poppy-smeared.
Sunlight surrounds me and winter birds
                              doodle and peck in the dead grass.
I'm emptied, ready to go. Again
I tell myself what I've told myself for almost thirty years—
Listen to John, do what the clouds do.

APPALACHIA

STRAY PARAGRAPHS IN FEBRUARY,
YEAR OF THE RAT

East of town, the countryside unwrinkles and smooths out
Unctuously toward the tidewater and gruff Atlantic.
A love of landscape's a true affection for regret, I've found,
Forever joined, forever apart,
                              outside us yet ourselves.

Renunciation, it's hard to learn, is now our ecstasy.
However, if God were still around,
                              he'd swallow our sighs in his nothingness.

The dregs of the absolute are slow sift in my blood,
Dead branches down after high winds, dead yard grass and
     undergrowth—
The sure accumulation of all that's not revealed
Rises like snow in my bare places,
                              cross-whipped and openmouthed.

Our lives can't be lived in flames.
Our lives can't be lit like saints' hearts,
                              seared between heaven and earth.

February, old head-turner, cut us some slack, grind of bone
On bone, such melancholy music.
Lift up that far corner of landscape,
                              there, toward the west.
Let some of the deep light in, the arterial kind.

STRAY PARAGRAPHS IN APRIL,
YEAR OF THE RAT

Only the dead can be born again, and then not much.
I wish I were a mole in the ground,
                                    eyes that see in the dark.

Attentive without an object of attentiveness,
Unhappy without an object of unhappiness—
Desire in its highest form,
                    dog prayer, diminishment . . .

If we were to walk for a hundred years, we could never take
One step toward heaven—
                    you have to wait to be gathered.

Two cardinals, two blood clots,
Cast loose in the cold, invisible arteries of the air.
If they ever stop, the sky will stop.

Affliction's a gift, Simone Weil thought—
The world becomes more abundant in severest light.

April, old courtesan, high-styler of months, dampen our mouths.

The dense and moist and cold and dark come together here.

The soul is air, and it maintains us.

BASIC DIALOGUE

The transformation of objects in space,
                                        or objects in time,
To objects outside either, but tactile, still precise . . .
It's always the same problem—
Nothing's more abstract, more unreal,
                                        than what we actually see.
The job is to make it otherwise.

Two dead crepe-myrtle bushes,
                            tulips petal-splayed and swan-stemmed,
All blossoms gone from the blossoming trees—the new loss
Is not like old loss,
Winter-kill, a jubilant revelation, an artificial thing
Linked and lifted by pure description into the other world.

Self-oblivion, sacred information, God's nudge—
I think I'll piddle around by the lemon tree, thorns
Sharp as angel's teeth.
                        I think
I'll lie down in the dandelions, the purple and white violets.
I think I'll keep on lying there, one eye cocked toward heaven.

April eats from my fingers,
                            nibble of dogwood, nip of pine.
Now is the time, Lord.
Syllables scatter across the new grass, in search of their words.
Such minor Armageddons.
Beside the waters of disremembering,
                                    I lay me down.

STAR TURN

Nothing is quite as secretive as the way the stars
Take off their bandages and stare out
At the night,
        that dark rehearsal hall,
And whisper their little songs,
The alpha and beta ones, the ones from the great fire.

Nothing is quite as gun shy,
        the invalid, broken pieces
Drifting and rootless, rising and falling, forever
Deeper into the darkness.
Nightly they give us their dumb show, nightly they flash us
Their message and melody,
        frost-sealed, our lidless companions.

A BAD MEMORY MAKES YOU A METAPHYSICIAN, A GOOD ONE MAKES YOU A SAINT

This is our world, high privet hedge on two sides,
                                half-circle of arborvitae,
Small strip of sloped lawn,
Last of the spring tulips and off-purple garlic heads
Snug in the cutting border,
Dwarf orchard down deep at the bottom of things,
                                God's crucible,
Bat-swoop and grab, grackle yawp, back yard . . .

This is our landscape,
Bourgeois, heartbreakingly suburban;
                                these are the ashes we rise from.
As night goes down, we watch it darken and disappear.
We push our glasses back on our foreheads,
                                look hard, and it disappears.

In another life, the sun shines and the clouds are motionless.
There, too, the would-be-saints are slipping their hair shirts on.
But only the light souls can be saved;
Only the ones whose weight
                                will not snap the angel's wings.
Too many things are not left unsaid.
If you want what the syllables want, just do your job.

THINKING ABOUT THE POET LARRY LEVIS
ONE AFTERNOON IN LATE MAY

Rainy Saturday, Larry dead
                    almost three weeks now,
Rain starting to pool in the low spots
And creases along the drive.
                              Between showers, the saying goes,
Roses and rhododendron wax glint
Through dogwood and locust leaves,
Flesh-colored, flesh-destined, spring in false flower, goodbye.

The world was born when the devil yawned,
                              the legend goes,
And who's to say it's not true,
Color of flesh, some inner and hidden bloom of flesh.
Rain back again, then back off,
Sunlight suffused like a chest pain across the tree limbs.
God, the gathering night, assumes it.

We haven't a clue as to what counts
In the secret landscape behind the landscape we look at here.
We just don't know what matters,
                              May dull and death-distanced,
Sky half-lit and grackle-ganged—
It's all the same dark, it's all the same absence of dark.
Part of the rain has now fallen, the rest still to fall.

IN THE KINGDOM OF THE PAST,
THE BROWN-EYED MAN IS KING

It's all so pitiful, really, the little photographs
Around the room of places I've been,
And me in them, the half-read books, the fetishes, this
Tiny arithmetic against the dark undazzle.
Who do we think we're kidding?

Certainly not our selves, those hardy perennials
We take such care of, and feed, who keep on keeping on
Each year, their knotty egos like bulbs
Safe in the damp and dreamy soil of their self-regard.
No way we bamboozle them with these

Shrines to the woebegone, ex votos and reliquary sites
One comes in on one's knees to,
The country of *what was*, the country of *what we pretended to be*,
Cruxes and intersections of all we'd thought was fixed.
There is no guilt like the love of guilt.

PASSING THE MORNING UNDER
THE SERENISSIMA

Noon sun big as a knuckle,
                          tight over Ponte S. Polo,
Unlike the sighting of Heraclitus the Obscure,
Who said it's the width of a man's foot.
Unable to take the full
                   "clarity" of his fellow man,
He took to the mountains and ate grasses and wild greens,
Aldo Buzzi retells us.

Sick, dropsical, he returned to the city and stretched out on the
    ground
And covered his body with manure .
To dry himself out.
                 After two days of cure, he died,
Having lost all semblance of humanity, and was devoured by dogs.
Known as "the weeping philosopher," he said one time,
The living and the dead, the waked and the sleeping, are the same.

Thus do we entertain ourselves on hot days, Aldo Buzzi,
Cees Nooteboom, Gustave Flaubert,
The flies and nameless little insects '
                   circling like God's angels
Over the candy dish and worn rug.
The sun, no longer knuckle or foot,
                   strays behind June's flat clouds.
Boats bring their wild greens and bottled water down the
    Republic's shade-splotched canals.

VENETIAN DOG

Bad day in Bellini country, Venetian dog high-stepper
Out of Carpaccio and down the street,

                    tail like a crozier
Over his ivory back.
A Baron Corvo bad day, you mutter, under your short breath.

Listen, my friend, everything works to our disregard.
Language, our common enemy, moves like the tide against us,
Fortune's heel upwind

                over Dogana's golden universe
High in the cloud-scratched and distant sky.

Six p.m. Sunday church bells
Flurry and circle and disappear like pigeon flocks,
Lost in the sunlight's fizzle and fall.
The stars move as well against us.

                        From pity, it sometimes seems.

So what's the body to do,

                  caught in its web of spidered flesh?
Venetian dog has figured his out, and stands his ground,
Bristled and hogbacked,
Barking in cadence at something that you and I can't see.

                              But

For us, what indeed, lying like S. Lorenzo late at night
On his brazier, lit from above by a hole in the sky,
From below by coals,

              his arm thrown up,
In Titian's great altarpiece, in supplication, what indeed?

IN THE VALLEY OF THE MAGRA

In June, above Pontrèmoli, high in the Lunigiana,
The pollen-colored chestnut blooms
                            sweep like a long cloth
Snapped open over the bunched treetops
And up the mountain as far as the almost-Alpine meadows.
At dusk, in the half-light, they appear
Like stars come through the roots of the great trees from another
    sky.
Or tears, with my glasses off.
                       Sometimes they seem like that
Just as the light fades and the darkness darkens for good.

Or that's the way I remember it when the afternoon thunderstorms
Tumble out of the Blue Ridge,
And distant bombardments muscle in
                         across the line
Like God's solitude or God's shadow,
The loose consistency of mortar and river stone
Under my fingers where I leaned out
Over it all,
          isolate farm lights
Starting to take the color on, the way I remember it . . .

RETURNED TO THE YAAK CABIN,
I OVERHEAR AN OLD GREEK SONG

Back at the west window, Basin Creek
Stumbling its mantra out in a slurred, midsummer monotone,
Sunshine in planes and clean sheets
Over the yarrow and lodgepole pine—
We spend our whole lives in the same place and never leave,
Pine squirrels and butterflies at work in a deep dither,
Bumblebee likewise, wind with a slight hitch in its get-along.

Dead heads on the lilac bush, daisies
Long-legged forest of stalks in a white throw across the field
Above the ford and deer path,
Candor of marble, candor of bone—
We spend our whole lives in the same place and never leave,
The head of Orpheus bobbing in the slatch, his song
Still beckoning from his still-bloody lips, bright as a bee's heart.

ARS POETICA II

I find, after all these years, I am a believer—
I believe what the thunder and lightning have to say;
I believe that dreams are real,
                       and that death has two reprisals;
I believe that dead leaves and black water fill my heart.

I shall die like a cloud, beautiful, white, full of nothingness.

The night sky is an ideogram,
                       a code card punched with holes.
It thinks it's the word of what's-to-come.
It thinks this, but it's only The Library of Last Resort,
The reflected light of The Great Misunderstanding.

God is the fire my feet are held to.

CICADA BLUE

I wonder what Spanish poets would say about this,
Bloodless, mid-August meridian,
Afternoon like a sucked-out, transparent insect shell,
Diffused, and tough to the touch.
Something about a labial, probably,
                              something about the blue.

St. John of the Cross, say, or St. Teresa of Avila.
Or even St. Thomas Aquinas,
Who said, according to some,
                    "All I have written seems like straw
Compared to what I have seen and what has been revealed to me."
Not Spanish, but close enough,
                    something about the blue.

Blue, I love you, blue, one of them said once in a different color,
The edged and endless
Expanse of nowhere and nothingness
                         hemmed as a handkerchief from here,
Cicada shell of hard light
Just under it, blue, I love you, blue . . .

We've tried to press God in our hearts the way we'd press a leaf
      in a book,
Afternoon memoried now,
                    sepia into brown,
Night coming on with its white snails and its ghost of the
      Spanish poet,
Poet of shadows and death.
Let's press him firm in our hearts, O blue, I love you, blue.

ALL LANDSCAPE IS ABSTRACT, AND TENDS TO REPEAT ITSELF

I came to my senses with a pencil in my hand
And a piece of paper in front of me.
                                    To the years
Before the pencil, O, I was the resurrection.
Still, who knows where the soul goes,
Up or down,
                    after the light switch is turned off, who knows?

It's late August, and prophets are calling their bears in.

The sacred is frightening to the astral body,
As is its absence.
                    We have to choose which fear is our consolation.
Everything comes *ex alto,*
We'd like to believe, the origin and the end, or
Non-origin and the non-end,
                                    each distant and inaccessible.

Over the Blue Ridge, the whisperer starts to whisper in tongues.

Remembered landscapes are left in me
The way a bee leaves its sting,
                                    hopelessly, passion-placed,
Untranslatable language.
Non-mystical, insoluble in blood, they act as an opposite
To the absolute, whose words are a solitude, and set to music.

All forms of landscape are autobiographical.

OPUS POSTHUMOUS

Possum work, world's windowlust, lens of the Byzantine—
Friday in Appalachia.
Hold on, old skeletal life,
                          there's more to come, if I hear right.
Still, even the brightest angel is darkened by time,
Even the sharpest machine
                          dulled and distanced by death.

Wick-end of August, wicked once-weight of summer's sink and
    sigh.

September now, set to set foot on the other side,
Hurricanes sprouting like daisy heads around her lap.
We know where she's been. We know
What big secret she keeps,
                          so dark and dungeoned, and wish her well,
Praying that she will whisper it to us
                          just once, just this once.

The secret of language is the secret of disease.

QUOTATIONS

Renoir, whose paintings I don't much like,
Says what survives of the artist is the feeling he gives by means
    of objects.
I do like that, however,
The feeling put in as much as the feeling received
To make a work distinctive,
Though I'm not sure it's true,

                 or even it's workable.

When Chekhov died, he died at dawn,

                 a large moth circling the lamp,
Beating its pressed wings.
Placed in a zinc casket, the corpse, labeled *Fresh Oysters*,
Was sent to Moscow in a freight car from Germany.
His last words were, *Has the sailor left?*
I am dying, Ich sterbe.

My breath is corrupt, my days are extinct, the graves are ready
    for me,
Job says. *They change the night into day—*
The light is short because of darkness . . .
I have said to corruption,

             thou art my father, to the worm,
Thou art my mother and my sister—
They shall go down to the bars of the pit,

               when our rest together is in the dust.

That's all. There's nothing left after that.

As Meng Chiao says,

For a while the dust weighs lightly on my cloak.

THE APPALACHIAN BOOK OF THE DEAD II

Late Saturday afternoon in Charlottesville.
Columbus Day,

Windless, remorseless Columbus Day,
Sunlight like Scotch tape
Stuck to the surfaces of west-worn magnolia leaves.
Children are playing their silly games
Behind the back yard,
toneless, bell-less Columbus Day.

Despair's a sweet meat I'd hang a fang in once or twice,
Given the go-ahead.
And where's October's golden and red,
Where is its puff of white smoke?
Another page torn off
The Appalachian Book of the Dead,
Indifferent silence of heaven,
Indifferent silence of the world.

Jerusalem, I say quietly, Jerusalem,
The altar of evening starting to spread its black cloth
In the eastern apse of things—
   the soul that desires to return *home*, desires its own destruction,
We know, which never stopped anyone,
The fear of it and dread of it on every inch of the earth,
Though light's still lovely in the west,
billowing, purple and scarlet-white.

INDIAN SUMMER II

As leaves fall from the trees, the body falls from the soul.
As memory signs transcendence, scales fall from the heart.
As sunlight winds back on its dark spool,
$\qquad\qquad\qquad$ November's a burn and an ache.

A turkey buzzard logs on to the late evening sky.
Residual blood in the oak's veins.
Sunday. Recycling tubs like flower bins at the curb.

Elsewhere, buried up to her armpits,
$\qquad\qquad\qquad$ someone is being stoned to death.
Elsewhere, transcendence searches for us.
Elsewhere, this same story is being retold by someone else.

The heavenly way has been lost,
$\qquad\qquad\qquad$ no use to look at the sky.
Still, the stars, autumnal stars, start to flash and transverberate.
The body falls from the soul, and the soul takes off,
$\qquad\qquad\qquad$ a wandering, moral drug.

This is an end without a story.
This is a little bracelet of flame around your wrist.
This is the serpent in the Garden,
$\qquad\qquad\qquad$ her yellow hair, her yellow hair.

We live in two landscapes, as Augustine might have said,

One that's eternal and divine,
$\qquad\qquad\qquad$ and one that's just the back yard,
Dead leaves and dead grass in November, purple in spring.

AUTUMN'S SIDEREAL, NOVEMBER'S A BALL AND CHAIN

After the leaves have fallen, the sky turns blue again,
Blue as a new translation of Longinus on the sublime.
We wink and work back from its edges.
                                        We walk around
Under its sequence of metaphors,
Looking immaculately up for the overlooked.
Or looking not so immaculately down for the same thing.

If there's nothing going on, there's no reason to make it up.
Back here, for instance, next to the cankered limbs of the plum
    trees,
We take a load off.
                        Hard frost on the grass blades and wild onion,
Invisibly intricate, so clear.
Pine needles in herringbone, dead lemon leaves, dead dirt.
The metaphysical world is meaningless today,

South wind retelling its autobiography
                                        endlessly
Through the white pines, somesuch and susurration, shhh, shhh . . .

THE WRITING LIFE

Give me the names for things, just give me their real names,
Not what we call them, but what
They call themselves when no one's listening—
At midnight, the moon-plated hemlocks like unstruck bells,
God wandering aimlessly elsewhere.

> Their names, their secret names.

December. Everything's black and brown. Or half-black and half-
    brown.
What's still alive puts its arms around me,

> amen from the evergreens

That want my heart on their ribbed sleeves.
Why can't I listen to them?

> Why can't I offer my heart up

To what's in plain sight and short of breath?

Restitution of the divine in a secular circumstance—
Page 10, The Appalachian Book of the Dead,

> the dog-eared one,

Pre-solstice winter light laser-beaked, sun over Capricorn,
Dead-leaf-and-ice-mix grunged on the sidewalk and driveway.
Short days. Short days. Dark soon the light overtakes.

> Stump of a hand.

REPLY TO WANG WEI

The dream of reclusive life, a strict, essential solitude,
Is a younger hermit's dream.
Tuesday, five days till winter, a cold, steady rain.
White hair, white heart. The time's upon us and no exit
East of the lotus leaves.
                    No exit, you said, and a cold, steady rain.

Indeed.
          All those walks by the river, all those goodbyes.
Willows shrink back to brown across Locust Avenue,
The mountains are frost and blue
                      and fellow travellers.
Give you peace, you said, freedom from ten thousand matters.
And asked again, does fame come only to the ancients?

At the foot of the southern mountains, white clouds pass without
    end,
You wrote one time in a verse.
                      They still do, and still without end.
That's it. Just wanted to let you know it hasn't changed—no out,
    no end,
And fame comes only to the ancients, and justly so,
Rain turning slowly to snow now then back into rain.

Everywhere everywhere, you wrote, something is falling,
The evening mist has no resting place.
What time we waste, wasting time.
                  Still, I sit still,
The mind swept clean in its secret shade,
Though no monk from any hill will ever come to call.

GIORGIO MORANDI AND THE TALKING
ETERNITY BLUES

Late April in January, seventy-some-odd degrees.
The entry of Giorgio Morandi in The Appalachian Book of the Dead
Begins here, without text, without dates—
A photograph of the master contemplating four of his objects,
His glasses pushed high on his forehead,

                his gaze replaced and pitiless.

The dove, in summer, coos sixty times a minute, one book says.
Hard to believe that,

            even in this unseasonable heat,
A couple of them appearing and silent in the bare tree
Above me.

       Giorgio Morandi doesn't blink an eye
As sunlight showers like sulphur grains across his face.

There is an end to language.

        There is an end to handing out the names of things,
Clouds moving south to north along the Alleghenies
And Blue Ridge, south to north on the wind.
Eternity, unsurprisingly, doesn't give this a take.
Eternity's comfortless, a rock and a hard ground.

Now starless, Madonnaless, Morandi
Seems oddly comforted by the lack of comforting,
A proper thing in its proper place,
Landscape subsumed, language subsumed,

              the shadow of God
Liquid and indistinguishable.

DRONE AND OSTINATO

Winter. Cold like a carved thing outside the window glass.
Silence of sunlight and ice dazzle.
                              Stillness of noon.
Dragon back of the Blue Ridge,
Landscape laid open like an old newspaper, memory into memory.

Our lives are like birds' lives, flying around, blown away.
We're bandied and bucked on and carried across the sky,
Drowned in the blue of the infinite,
                              blur-white and drift.
We disappear as stars do, soundless, without a trace.

Nevertheless, let's settle and hedge the bet.
                              The wind picks up, clouds cringe,
Snow locks in place on the lawn.
Wordless is what the soul wants, the one thing that I keep in mind.
One in one united, bare in bare doth shine.

OSTINATO AND DRONE

> *The mystic's vision is beyond the world of individuation,*
> *it is beyond speech and thus incommunicable.*
> —PAUL MENDES-FLOHR, *Ecstatic Confessions*

Undoing the self is a hard road.
Somewhere alongside a tenderness that's infinite,
I gather, and loneliness that's infinite.
                                        No finitude.
There's nothing that bulks up in between.
Radiance. Unending brilliance of light
                        like drops of fire through the world.
Speechless. Incommunicable. At one with the one.

Some dead end—no one to tell it to,
                                nothing to say it with.
That being the case, I'd like to point out this quince bush,
Quiescent and incommunicado in winter shutdown.
I'd like you to notice its long nails
And skeletal underglow.
                        I'd like you to look at its lush
Day-dazzle, noon light and shower shine.

It's reasonable to represent anything that really exists
                        by that thing which doesn't exist,
Daniel Defoe said.
And that's what we're talking about, the difference between the
        voice and the word,
The voice continuing to come back in splendor,
                                the word still not forthcoming.
We're talking about the bush on fire.
We're talking about this quince bush, its noonday brilliance of light.

"IT'S TURTLES ALL THE WAY DOWN"

I snap the book shut. February. Alternate sky.
Tiny gobbets like pyracantha beans on the mock crab-apple trees.
None of this interests me.

Mercy is made of fire, and fire needs fire, another book says.
It also says, to get to God, pull both your feet back—
One foot from out of this life, one foot from the other.

Outside, I walk off-cadence under the evergreens,
Ground needles bronzed and half mythic, as though from a tomb,
5:20 winter lightfall sifted and steeped through medium yellow.

What God is the God behind the God who moves the chess pieces,
Borges wondered.
                    What mask is the mask behind the mask
The language wears and the landscape wears, I ask myself.

O, well, I let the south wind blow all over my face.
I let the sunshine release me and fall all over my face.
I try not to think of them stopping.

HALF FEBRUARY

St. Valentine's. Winter is in us.
Hard to be faithful to summer's bulge and buzz
$\qquad$ in such a medicine.
Hard to be heart-wrung
And sappy in what's unworkable and world-weary.
Hard to be halt and half-strung.

All of us, more or less, are unfaithful to something.
Solitude bears us away,
Approaches us in the form of a crescent, like love,
And bears us away
Into its icy comforting, our pain and our happiness.

I saw my soul like a little silkworm, diligently fed,
Spinning a thread with its little snout,
Anna Garcias wrote in the sixteenth century.
And who can doubt her,
Little silkworm in its nonbeing and nothingness.

Nothing like that in these parts these days—
The subject for today, down here, is the verb "to be,"
Snow falling, then sleet, then freezing rain,
St. Catherine nowhere in evidence, her left side opened, her heart
    removed,
All the world's noise, all its hubbub and din,
$\qquad$ now chill and a glaze.

BACK YARD BOOGIE WOOGIE

I look out at the back yard—
                    sur le motif, as Paul Cézanne would say,
Nondescript blond winter grass,
Boxwood buzz-cut still dormant with shaved sides, black gum tree
And weeping cherry veined and hived against the afternoon sky.

I try to look at landscape as though I weren't there,
                              but know, wherever I am,
I disturb that place by breathing, by my heart's beating—
I only remember things that I think I've forgot,
Lives the color of dead leaves, for instance, days like dead insects.

Most of my life is like that,
                    scattered, fallen, overlooked.
Back here, magenta rosettes flock the limbs of the maple trees,
Little thresholds of darkness,
Late February sunlight indifferent as water to all the objects in it.

Only perfection is sufficient, Simone Weil says.
Whew . . .
              Not even mercy or consolation can qualify.
Good thing I've got this early leaf bristle in my hand.
Good thing the cloud shadows keep on keeping on, east-by-
     northeast.

THE APPALACHIAN BOOK OF THE DEAD III

Full moon illuminated large initial for letter M,
Appalachian Book of the Dead, 22 February 1997—
La luna piove, the moon rains down its antibiotic light
Over the sad, septic world,
Hieroglyphs on the lawn, supplicant whispers for the other side,
I am pure, I am pure, I am pure . . .

The soul is in the body as light is in the air,
Plotinus thought.

          Well, I wouldn't know about that, but
La luna piove, and shines out in every direction—
Under it all, disorder, above,
A handful of stars on one side, a handful on the other.
Whatever afflictions we have, we have them for good.

Such Egyptology in the wind, such raw brushstrokes,
Moon losing a bit from its left side at two o'clock.
Still, light mind-of-Godish,

               silent deeps where seasons don't exist.
Surely some splendor's set to come forth,
Some last equation solved, declued and reclarified.
South wind and a long shine, a small-time paradiso . . .

OPUS POSTHUMOUS II

Sitting as though suspended from something, cool in my deck chair,
Unlooked-on, otherworldly.
There is no acquittal, there is no body of light and elegy.
There is no body of fire.

It is as though an angel had walked across the porch,
A conflagration enhanced, extinguished, then buried again,
No pardon, no nourishment.
It's March, and starvelings feed from my mouth.

Ubi amor, ibi oculus,
                              love sees what the eye sees
Repeatedly, more or less.
It certainly seems so here, the gates of the arborvitae
The gates of mercy look O look they feed from my mouth.

BODY LANGUAGE

The human body is not the world, and yet it is.
The world contains it, and is itself contained. Just so.
The distance between the two
Is like the distance between the *no* and the *yes*,

                        abysmal distance,
Nothing and everything. Just so.

This morning I move my body like a spring machine
Among the dormant and semi-dead,
The shorn branches and stubbed twigs

                       hostile after the rain,
Grumpy and tapped out as go-betweens.
Blossoming plum tree coronal toast, cankered and burned.

When body becomes the unbody,
Look hard for its certitude, inclusive, commensurate thing.
Look for its lesson and camouflage.
Look hard for its leash point and linkup.
The shadow of the magnolia tree is short shrift for the grass.

I move through the afternoon,

                    autumnal in pre-spring,
October-headed, hoarfrost-fingered.
The body inside the body is the body I want to come to—
I see it everywhere,
Lisping and licking itself, breaking and entering.

"WHEN YOU'RE LOST IN JUAREZ, IN THE RAIN, AND IT'S EASTERTIME TOO"

Like a grain of sand added to time,
Like an inch of air added to space,
                              or a half-inch,
We scribble our little sentences.
Some of them sound okay and some of them sound not so okay.
A grain and an inch, a grain and an inch and a half.

Sad word wands, desperate alphabet.

Still, there's been no alternative
Since language fell from the sky.
Though mystics have always said that communication is languageless.
And maybe they're right—
                              the soul speaks and the soul receives.
Small room for rebuttal there . . .

Over the Blue Ridge, late March late light annunciatory and
    visitational.

Tonight, the comet Hale-Bopp
                              will ghost up on the dark page of the sky
By its secret juice and design from the full moon's heat.
Tonight, some miracle will happen somewhere, it always does.
Good Friday's a hard rain that won't fall,
Wild onion and clump grass, green on green.

Our mouths are incapable, white violets cover the earth.

THE APPALACHIAN BOOK OF THE DEAD IV

High-fiving in Charlottesville.
Sunset heaped up, as close to us as a barrel fire.
Let's all go down to the river,
                    there's a man there that's walking on the water,
On the slow, red Rivanna,
He can make the lame walk, he can make the dumb talk,
                    and open up the eyes of the blind.
That dry-shod, over-the-water walk.

Harbor him in your mind's eye, snub him snug to your hearts.

They'll have to sing louder than that.
                    They'll have to dig deeper into the earbone
For this one to get across.
They'll have to whisper a lot about the radiant body.
Murmur of river run, murmur of women's voices.
Raised up, without rhyme,
                    the murmur of women's voices.
Good luck was all we could think to say.

Dogwood electrified and lit from within by April afternoon late-light.

This is the lesson for today—
                    narrative, narrative, narrative . . .
Tomorrow the sun comes back.
Tomorrow the tailings and slush piles will turn to gold
When everyone's down at the river.
The muscadines will bring forth,
The mountain laurel and jack-in-heaven,
                    while everyone's down at the river.

SPRING STORM

After the rainfall, a little Buddha in each water drop,
After the rainfall, a little rainbow in each one,
Sun like a one-eyed, Venetian Doge
        checking it out,
Then letting the clouds slide shut.
The Chinese can guide you to many things,
        but the other side's not one of them,
Water reflecting sun's fire, then not.

And the stars keep on moving—
        no one can tie them to one place.
Doge eye from under the cloud, sky mullioned with oak limbs,
Stars moving unseen behind the light surge, great river.
The end of desire is the beginning of wisdom,
We keep on telling ourselves,
      lone crow
In sun-splotch now crawling across the lawn, black on black.

EARLY SATURDAY AFTERNOON, EARLY EVENING

Saturday. Early afternoon. High
Spring light through new green,
                a language, it seems, I have forgotten,
But which I'll remember soon enough
When the first pages are turned
                in The Appalachian Book of the Dead.
The empty ones. The ones about the shining and stuff.

Father darkness, mother abyss,
                the shadow whispered,
Abolish me, make me light.
And so it happened. Rumor of luminous bodies.
The face on the face of the water became no face.
The words on the page of the book became a hush.
                And luminous too.

These things will come known to you,
                these things make soft your shift,
Alliteration of lost light, aspirate hither-and-puff,
Afternoon undervoices starting to gather and lift off
In the dusk,
        Red Rover, Red Rover, let Billy come over,
Laughter and little squeals, a quick cry.

"THE HOLY GHOST ASKETH FOR US WITH MOURNING AND WEEPING UNSPEAKABLE"

Well, sainthood's a bottomless pity,
                              as some wag once said, so
Better forget about that.
I'd rather, in any case, just sit here and watch the rose bleed.
I'd rather it it than me.
For that's how the world proceeds, I've found out,
                              some blood and a lot of *watch*.

Still, I like to think of them there in their gold gowns and hair shirts,
Missing whatever was lost or lopped
Their last time around,
                              its absence revealing a pride of place.
I like to think of their tender flesh
Just healed, or just beginning to heal,
                              syrupy, sweet like that.

Whatever has been will be again,
                              unaltered, ever-returning.
Serenity of the rhododendron, pink and white,
Dark cinnamon, pink and white,
Azaleas opening in their own deep sleep. Ours too.
After-rupture of tulip border, and
                              white light in the green.

Unseen, unlistened to, unspoken of.
                              Salvation.
Light is, light is not, light is—
However you look at it, the heaven of the contemplatives is a hard gig.
Thrones and Dominions they'd drift among.
The landscape and wild chestnut will not remember them.

THE APPALACHIAN BOOK OF THE DEAD V

Half-asleep on the back deck,
                              low wasp-hum of power mower
Ebbing and coming back from next door,
Aggressive shadows of maple leaves
                              crabbing across the shy sunlight
Languishing apprehensively over the fresh-stained pine boards.
Half-silence, 5 p.m. traffic tide, half-silence, violin tone scales.

So, where do we go from here,
Indoors now, great rush of wheels in my head, it is spring—
Vacancy, earth life, remains out there,
                              somewhere in the machine.
Waiting for something to come—anything—and mushroom,
I think of myself as a hare, as Virginia Woolf once said,
                              stilled, expecting moon-visitors.

When your answers have satisfied the forty-two gods,
When your heart's in balance with the weight of a feather,
When your soul is released like a sibyl from its cage,
Like a wind you'll cross over,
                              not knowing how, not knowing where,
Remembering nothing, unhappening, hand and foot.

The world's a glint on the window glass,
The landscape's a flash and fall,
                              sudden May rain like a sleet spill
On the tin roof, no angel, night dark.
Eternity puddles up.
And here's the Overseer, blue, and O he is blue . . .

STAR TURN II

How small the stars are tonight, bandannaed by moonlight,
How few and how far between—
Disordered and drained, like highlights in Dante's death mask.
Or a sequined dress from the forties
                              —hubba-hubba—
Some sequins missing, some sequins inalterably in place.

Unlike our lives, which are as they are.
Unlike our imagined selves, which are as we'll never become,
Star-like and shining,
Everyone looking up at, everyone pointing there, O there,
Masked and summering in,
              each one a bright point, each one a dodged eclipse.

AFTER READING T'AO CH'ING, I WANDER UNTETHERED THROUGH THE SHORT GRASS

Dry spring, no rain for five weeks.
Already the lush green begins to bow its head and sink to its knees.

Already the plucked stalks and thyroid weeds like insects
Fly up and trouble my line of sight.

I stand inside the word *here*

                          as that word stands in its sentence,
Unshadowy, half at ease.

Religion's been in a ruin for over a thousand years.
Why shouldn't the sky be tatters,

                                lost notes to forgotten songs?

I inhabit who I am, as T'ao Ch'ing says, and walk about
Under the mindless clouds.

                         When it ends, it ends. What else?

One morning I'll leave home and never find my way back—
My story and I will disappear together, just like this.

REMEMBERING SPELLO, SITTING OUTSIDE IN PRAMPOLINI'S GARDEN

In and out of the shy, limp leaves of the grape arbor,
Song birds slither and peel back.

High in the Umbrian sky, the ghosts
Of true saints pinwheel and congregate like pale, afternoon
    clouds
Ready to jump-start the universe,

The Gates of Propertius—so they say—
                       cream-porphyry at the west of town,
Monte Subasio north-northwest.

It's getting late. The white dog has buried her bits of bread and
The early apricots start to shine,
                     forty-watt bulbs
Against the sundowned and mottled plain.

No word for time, no word for God, landscape exists outside
    each,
But stays, incurable ache, both things,

And bears me out as evening darkens and steps forth,
                      my body snug in my life
As a gun in its carrying case,
As an old language, an old address.

I sit in my plastic lawn chair,
                 unearthly and dispossessed,
My eyes on the turning stars.
Like a Roman statue, I watch everything and see nothing.

Just under the surface of the earth,
The traffic continues to glide by
                    all night with its lights off.

AFTER REREADING ROBERT GRAVES, I GO OUTSIDE TO GET MY HEAD TOGETHER

Fourth of July. A stillness across the morning like
The inside of the inside of a hot, uncomforting place.
Head-hunting sky, high clouds lingering, half-suggestive,
Mare's-tailed and double layered.
Green leaves. Clouds and sky. Green leaves. Clouds. Sky.

According to Graves, the true function of poetry
Is a strict, religious invocation of the Muse.
Tell it to the Marines, Roberto,
                              the Muse is as dead as God is.
In memory of the Muse, perhaps—
In memory of a Memory: a hidden face, a long, white veil.

And yet The Appalachian Book of the Dead exists,
In part, to ease an exit, praise the present and praise the past,
To click the abacus beads, to sum their cloudy count.
(Though sometimes subtraction seems the thing,
A little less of this, a little less of all that.)

Early summer, idle images. No wind, no wound,
The world unpetaled and opened to anyone's tongue.
My next-door neighbor's lawn sprinkler crests and collapses beyond the
      hedge,
A cardinal taunts me from her branch.
                              Now bees drag their wet loads
Across the garden to feed their queen, huge in her humming hive.

AMERICAN TWILIGHT

Why do I love the sound of children's voices in unknown games
So much on a summer's night,
Lightning bugs lifting heavily out of the dry grass
Like alien spacecraft looking for higher ground,
Darkness beginning to sift like coffee grains
                              over the neighborhood?

Whunk of a ball being kicked,
Surf-suck and surf-spill from traffic along the bypass,
American twilight,
                  Venus just lit in the third heaven,
Time-tick between "Okay, let's go," and "This earth is not my home."

Why do I care about this? Whatever happens will happen
With or without us,
                  with or without these verbal amulets.
In the first ply, in the heaven of the moon, a little light,
Half-light, over Charlottesville.
Trees reshape themselves, the swallows disappear, lawn sprinklers
    do the wave.

Nevertheless, it's still summer: cicadas pump their boxes,
Jack Russell terriers, as they say, start barking their heads off,
And someone, somewhere, is putting his first foot, then the second,
Down on the other side,
                no hand to help him, no tongue to wedge its weal.

THE APPALACHIAN BOOK OF THE DEAD VI

Last page, The Appalachian Book of the Dead,

full moon,

No one in anyone's arms, no lip to ear, cloud bank
And boyish soprano out of the east edge of things.
Ball-whomp and rig-grind stage right,
Expectancy, quivering needle, at north-northwest.

And here comes the angel with her drum and wings. Some wings.
Lost days, as Meng Chiao says, a little window of words
We peer through darkly. Darkly,
Moon stopped in cloud bank, light slick for the chute and long slide,
No lip, no ear.

Distant murmur of women's voices.

I hear that the verb is facilitate. To facilitate.
Azure. To rise. To rise through the azure. Illegible joy.
No second heaven. No first.
I think I'll lie here like this awhile, my back flat on the floor.
I hear that days bleed.

I hear that the right word will take your breath away.

LANDSCAPE AS METAPHOR,
LANDSCAPE AS FATE AND A HAPPY LIFE

August. Montana. The black notebook open again.
Across the blue-veined, dune-flattened, intimate blank of the page,
An almost-unseeable winged insect has set forth
On foot.
        I think I'll track his white trail.

—To set one's mind on the ink-line, to set one's heart on the dark
Unknowable, is far and forlorn, wouldn't you say?

Up here, our lives continue to lift off like leaf spores in the noon-wash,
Spruce trees and young hemlocks stand guard like Egyptian dogs
At the mouth of the meadow,
Butterflies flock like angels,
               and God knees our necks to the ground.

—Nevertheless, the stars at midnight blow in the wind like high
    cotton.
There is no place in the world they don't approach and pass over.

Wind lull, midmorning, tonight's sky
                  light-shielded, monkish and grand
Behind the glare's iconostasis, yellow poppies
Like lip prints against the log wall, the dead sister's lunar words
Like lip prints against it, this is as far as it goes . . .

—The sun doesn't shine on the same dog's back every day.
Only you, Fragrant One, are worthy to judge us and move on.

OPUS POSTHUMOUS III

Mid-August meltdown, Assurbanipal in the west,
Scorched cloud-towers, crumbling thrones—
The ancients knew to expect a balance at the end of things,
The burning heart against the burning feather of truth.
                                                    Sweet-mouthed,
Big ibis-eyed, in the maple's hieroglyphs, I write it down.

All my life I've looked for this slow light, this smallish light
Starting to seep, coppery blue,
                    out of the upper right-hand corner of things,
Down through the trees and off the back yard,
Rising and falling at the same time, now rising, now falling,
Inside the lapis lazuli of late afternoon.

Until the clouds stop, and hush.
Until the left hedge and the right hedge,
                                the insects and short dogs,
The back porch and barn swallows grain-out and disappear.
Until the bypass is blown with silence, until the grass grieves.
Until there is nothing else.

NORTH AMERICAN BEAR

STEP-CHILDREN OF PARADISE

Dark of the moon, bear's tail through triage of winter trees,
Back yard a deep
     tabula rasa, where to begin?

With or without language, there's always room for another life.
We've downloaded this one into an anxious indeterminacy,
Doing a little of this and a little of that,
As time, the true dissolver, eats away at our fingertips,
Leaving us memory and its end game,
       blurred star chart in the black light.

When the world has disappeared, someone will have to carry us,
Unseen and nightlong.
      When the world has disappeared, amigo,
Somebody's got to pick up the load.
Rainy Saturday, January doldrums, toothache
Like a saint's call in my mouth, unavoidable, up and down.

We live our lives like stars, unconstellated stars, just next to
Great form and great structure,
       ungathered, uncalled upon.

FREEZING RAIN

Cold snare taps on the skylight,
                              ice like a new conk on the trees,
Winter's slick-back and stiff gel,
Streetlamp reflections like vogueing boys
                              doing the neighborhood.

Unlike the stars, herded together in their dark yard,
Programmed, unalterable,
                              outriders sketched and firmed in.
Unlike their processed and guttering constellations.

There is an order beyond form,
                              but not there. Not here, either.

THINKING ABOUT THE NIGHT SKY,
I REMEMBER A POEM BY TU FU

Drifting, drifting, a single gull between sky and earth,
He said of himself, alone at night on the Yangtze,
Bent grasses and gentle wind.
                              And asked where his name was
Among the poets.
                    No answer, moon's disk on the great river.

People have free-fallen for thousands of miles through the distances
        of the heart,
Snowfall like starbursts
                        in the porch light's snap and slow freeze.
Such big flakes, such sure descent.
Black window of night behind the arborvitae,
                              bright grass and slender brocade.

Where there's smoke, there's ash.
                              Useless to let the mind grind down
To what's beyond it.
I'll set my sights on something small. I'll finish this poem,
This one that's not about the stars,
                        but what's between them.

NORTH AMERICAN BEAR

Early November in the soul,
                      a hard rain, and dusky gold
From the trees, late afternoon
Squint-light and heavy heart-weight.
It's always downleaf and dim.
A sixty-two-year-old, fallow-voiced, night-leaning man,
I stand at ease on the blank sidewalk.
Unhinder my habitat, starlight, make me insoluble;
Negative in my afterscape,
                     sidle the shadow across my mouth.

———

Random geometry of the stars,
                      random word-strings
As beautiful as the alphabet.
Or so I remember them,
                 North American Bear,
Orion, Cassiopeia and the Pleiades,
Stitching their syntax across the deep North Carolina sky
A half-century ago,
The lost language of summer nights, the inarticulate scroll
Of time
          pricked on its dark, celestial cylinder.

———

What is it about the stars we can't shake?
                   What pulse, what tide drop
Pulls us like vertigo upward, what
Height-like reversal urges us toward their clear deeps?

Tonight, for instance,
Something is turning behind my eyes,
                              something unwept, something unnamable,
Spinning its line out.
Who is to say the hijacked heart has not returned to its cage?
Who is to say some angel has not
                              breathed in my ear?

————

I walk in the chill of the late autumn night
                              like Orpheus,
Thinking my song, anxious to look back,
My vanished life an ornament, a drifting cloud, behind me,
A soft, ashen transcendence
Buried and resurrected once, then time and again.
The sidewalk unrolls like a deep sleep.
Above me the stars, stern stars,
Uncover their faces.
                    No heartbeat on my heels, no footfall.

————

The season approaches us, dead leaves and withered grasses
Waxed by the wind wherever you look,
                              the clear night sky
Star-struck and star-stung, that constellation, those seven high stars,
General Ke-Shu lifting his sword, the Chinese say.
Or one of them said,
One at the Western Front as part of his army, without doubt.
I almost can see him myself,
                    long-sword over the Bear's neck,
His car wheel-less, darkness sifting away like a sandstorm to the west.

Some of these star fires must surely be ash by now.
I dawdle outside in the back yard,
Humming old songs that no one cares about anymore.
The hat of darkness tilts the night sky
Inch by inch, foot by black foot,

over the Blue Ridge.
How bright the fire of the world was, I think to myself,
Before white hair and the ash of days.
I gaze at the constellations,

forgetting whatever it was I had to say.

———

The sidewalk again, unrolling grey and away. 9 p.m.
A cold wind from the far sky.
There is a final solitude I haven't arrived at yet,
Weariness like a dust in my throat.

I simmer inside its outline,
However, and feel safe, as the stars spill by, for one more night
Like some medieval journeyman enfrescoed with his poem in his hand,
Heaven remaining my neighborhood.
And like him, too, with something red and inviolate

under my feet.

IF YOU TALK THE TALK, YOU BETTER WALK THE WALK

The Buddhist monk hears all past
                 and all future in one stroke of the temple bell,
And pries the world out from a pinpoint.
Or grinds it down from immensity to a wheat grain.
Those are his footprints, there by the monastery wall.
This is the life he rejected, written around us—

Incessant rain, slip-stitch vocabulary of winter trees
And winter dreadlocks on half-abandoned garden stalks
Long deconstructed, so
                 familiar and comforting
We don't understand a word.
Another February morning at the heart of the world.

The country we live in's illegible, impossible of access.
We climb, like our deepest selves, out of it forever.
Upward, we think, but who knows.
                 Are those lights stars or the flametips of hell?
Who knows. We dig in and climb back up.
Wind shear and sleight-of-hand, hard cards, we keep on climbing.

ST. AUGUSTINE AND THE ARCTIC BEAR

China moon in the northeast, egg-like, 9:10 p.m.
There is no story here, only the moon
                         and a few script-stars,
Everything headed due west on its way through heaven,
Constellations like silver combs with their shell inlays,
Darkness like a sweet drink on the tongue.

No story, perhaps, but something's trying to get told,
Though not by me.
                 Augustine said that neither future
Nor past exists, as one is memory, the other expectation.
When expectation becomes memory, I'd hasten to add,
We'll live in the past, a cold house on a dark street.

However, he also said,
None fall who will lift their eyes.
And said that time, in essence, remains a body without form.
On the other hand, the arctic bear,
Like time invisible in its element,
                   has form to burn,

But does not do so, and keeps his eyes
                     fixed on the black water.
As I do, wherever I find it,
Bubba's bateau and his long pole
                always at my back,
A lap and a noisome breeze.
Formless and timeless, he wears my heart on his hard sleeve.

SKY DIVING

Clear night after four days' rain,
     moon brushed and blanched, three-quarters full.
Arterial pulse of ground lights and constellations.

I've talked about one thing for thirty years,
      and said it time and again,
Wind like big sticks in the trees—
I mean the still, small point at the point where all things meet;
I mean the form that moves the sun and the other stars.

What a sidereal jones we have!
     Immensity fills us
Like moonrise across the night sky, the dark disappears,
Worlds snuff, nothing acquits us,
And still we stand outside and look up,
     look up at the heavens and think,

Such sidebars, such extra-celestial drowning pools
To swallow us.
   Let's lie down together. Let's open our mouths.

NOTES

READING RORTY AND PAUL CELAN ONE MORNING IN EARLY JUNE
Contingency, Irony and Solidarity, Richard Rorty (1989).

AFTER READING TU FU, I GO OUTSIDE TO THE DWARF ORCHARD
Three Hundred Poems of the T'ang Dynasty, translator(s) anonymous (undated).

THINKING OF DAVID SUMMERS AT THE BEGINNING OF WINTER
"Pliny's outline": Pliny said the invention of painting occurred when a Corinthian maiden drew the outline of her lover after he went away to war, so she could remember what he looked like.

CICADA
The Confessions of Saint Augustine, translated by R. S. Pine-Coffin (1961); *One Hundred Poems from the Chinese*, Kenneth Rexroth (1956).

SPRUNG NARRATIVES
Real Presences, George Steiner (1989).

BLAISE PASCAL LIP-SYNCS THE VOID
Pensées, Blaise Pascal, translated by A. J. Krailsheimer (1966).

WINTER-WORSHIP
The Songlines, Bruce Chatwin (1988).

EAST OF THE BLUE RIDGE, OUR TOMBS ARE IN THE DOVE'S THROAT
Collected Poems: Federico García Lorca, ed. Christopher Maurer (1991).

ABSENCE INSIDE AN ABSENCE
"The Apophatic Image: The Poetics of Effacement in Julian of Norwich," Vincent Gillespie and Maggie Ross, in *The Medieval Mystical Tradition in England* (unpublished).

WITH SIMIC AND MARINETTI AT THE GIUBBE ROSSE
The Giubbe Rosse is a caffè in Florence, Italy.

WAITING FOR TU FU

The Selected Poems of Tu Fu, translated by David Hinton (1989); *Poems of Paul Celan*, translated by Michael Hamburger (1988).

STILL LIFE WITH STICK AND WORD

Natura Morta, Giorgio Morandi, *c.* 1957, The University of Iowa Museum of Art; "Full of Feeling IV," Tu Fu, *Bright Moon, Perching Bird*, translated by Seaton and Cryer (1987).

SUMMER STORM

Composition in Gray and Red, 1935, Piet Mondrian, The Art Institute of Chicago.

LOOKING ACROSS LAGUNA CANYON AT DUSK, WEST-BY-NORTHWEST

The Marriage of Cadmus and Harmony, Roberto Calasso, translated by Tim Parks (1993).

APOLOGIA PRO VITA SUA

The Nag Hammadi Library, James M. Robinson, general editor (1988).

LIVES OF THE SAINTS

Walter Raleigh, Gertrude Stein, Wallace Stevens, Dante Alighieri, Adam Gopnik, Bertran de Born, Donald Justice, Robert Graves, Anonymous (early thirteenth century).

LIVES OF THE ARTISTS

The Poems of Sappho, translated by Suzy Q Groden (1966); *The Nag Hammadi Library; Lives of the Artists*, Giorgio Vasari, translated by George Bull (1965).

THINKING OF WINTER AT THE BEGINNING OF SUMMER

Jacques Prévert, "Picasso's Walk."

BLACK ZODIAC

The Ruin of Kasch, Roberto Calasso, translated by William Weaver and Stephen Sartarelli (1994); *The Confessions* of St. Augustine, translated by R. S. Pine-Coffin (1961); *Poems of Paul Celan*, translated by Michael Hamburger (1989); "Adagia," Wallace Stevens, from *Opus Posthumous* (1957).

CHINA MAIL

The poems of Tu Fu, various translators.

DISJECTA MEMBRA
("These fragments are the *disjecta membra* of an elusive, coveted, and vaguely scented knowledge." Guido Ceronetti, *The Silence of the Body*); *Poems of the Late T'ang*, translated by A. C. Graham (1965); Letters of Paul Celan to Nelly Sachs; *The Nag Hammadi Library; Poems of Paul Celan.*

STRAY PARAGRAPHS IN APRIL, YEAR OF THE RAT
Simone Weil's notebooks.

A BAD MEMORY MAKES YOU A METAPHYSICIAN, A GOOD ONE MAKES YOU A SAINT
The title as well as two lines in the text have been taken and laundered from material in E. M. Cioran's *Tears and Saints*, translated by Ilinca Zarifopol-Johnston (1995).

IN THE VALLEY OF THE MAGRA
Gerard Manley Hopkins, *The Poems of Gerard Manley Hopkins*, 4th edition, "In the Valley of the Elwy" (1970).

ALL LANDSCAPE IS ABSTRACT, AND TENDS TO REPEAT ITSELF
Guido Ceronetti, *The Silence of the Body*, translated by Michael Moore (1993).

AUTUMN'S SIDEREAL, NOVEMBER'S A BALL AND CHAIN
Wallace Stevens, *Collected Poems of Wallace Stevens* "Jonga," (1965).

REPLY TO WANG WEI
Poems of Wang Wei, translated by G. W. Robinson (1973).

DRONE AND OSTINATO
Ecstatic Confessions (Meister Eckhart), compiled by Martin Buber, edited by Paul Mendes-Flohr (1985).

OSTINATO AND DRONE
Ibid.

HALF FEBRUARY
Ibid. Thomas Merton/Czeslaw Milosz, *Striving Towards Being*, edited by Robert Faggen (1997).

BACK YARD BOOGIE WOOGIE
Simone Weil, *Waiting for God*, translated by Emma Craufurd (1973).

OPUS POSTHUMOUS II
Ezra Pound, "Canto 90," *The Cantos* (1970).

"WHEN YOU'RE LOST IN JUAREZ, IN THE RAIN, AND IT'S EASTERTIME TOO"
(SIC)
Bob Dylan; I. M. Pei.

THE APPALACHIAN BOOK OF THE DEAD IV
Mac Wiseman, "Let's All Go Down to the River" (trad.).

SPRING STORM
Gary Snyder, *Mountains and Rivers Without End* (1996).

THE APPALACHIAN BOOK OF THE DEAD V
The Diaries of Virginia Woolf.

AFTER READING T'AO CH'ING . . .
The Selected Poems of T'ao Ch'ing, translated by David Hinton.

THINKING ABOUT THE NIGHT SKY, I REMEMBER A POEM BY TU FU
Li Po and Tu Fu, translated by Arthur Cooper (1973).

NORTH AMERICAN BEAR
Three Hundred Poems of the T'ang Dynasty, translator(s) anonymous (undated); "Orpheus, Euridyce and Hermes," Rainer Maria Rilke/Robert Lowell, *Imitations* (1995).

IF YOU TALK THE TALK, YOU BETTER WALK THE WALK
Poems of the Late T'ang, translated by A. C. Graham (1965) (Li Shang-Yiu, "Written on a Monastery Wall").

CPSIA information can be obtained at www.ICGtesting.com
Printed in the USA
LVOW06s1525160714

394634LV00002B/333/P